THE BRIDGE STUDENT TEXT

VOLUME 4 — DEFENSE AT CONTRACT BRIDGE

by Randall Baron and Frank Stewart

Drawings by Jude Goodwin

Published by
Devyn Press, Inc.
Louisville,
Kentucky

Dedications

To C. H.
F. S.

To Mary, Devyn and Dustin.
R. S. B.

Acknowledgments

Grateful thanks to:
Betty Mattison for her patience and typesetting skills;
Pat Houington, Tony Lipka and Henry Francis for their editorial
    assistance;
Izzy Ellis and V.B.I. for their cover photography;
also to Mimi Maier and Bonnie Baron Pollack.

The reader is referred to as "he" to make the text more readable.

Printed in the United States of America.

Devyn Press, Inc.
3600 Chamberlain Lane, Suite 230
Louisville, KY 40241

ISBN 0-910791-54-6

Table of Contents

Introduction

This text will help you get the most from your bridge course. It includes a summary of each lesson, plus quizzes so you may test your understanding of the material. If you learn everything this text has to offer, you'll be ready for anyone at the bridge table!

Since actual play has no substitute as a learning experience, try to play bridge outside class as much as possible. We also encourage you to read other books and check out the bridge column in your local newspaper. You cannot become a fine player in only 20 hours of class time.

The rewards of mastering this game are most satisfying. You will have a stimulating way of entertaining yourself and a way of making friends wherever you go. If you are more ambitious, organized tournament competition can lead to a world championship!

Good luck. Enjoy yourself.

Lesson 1

COUNT YOUR TRICKS!
DEFENDING ON AN ASSUMPTION

This lesson deals with two simple concepts that turn up in almost every deal you defend.

I. COUNT YOUR TRICKS. Just as a good declarer always counts sure winners and potential losers in planning the play, the *defenders should try to count their possible tricks* when they see dummy. It is easier to count defensive tricks when the contract is a game or slam — then your options will be limited. In a part-score the play may have to develop before you know where your tricks will come from. Counting winners on defense often tells you what you must do to defeat the contract. If you ask yourself, "Where will the setting trick come from?" there may be only one possible answer.

II. DEFENDING ON AN ASSUMPTION. It pays to be an optimist on defense! To count enough tricks to set the contract, you may have to *assume* that partner, or declarer, has a specific holding. This is called *defending on an assumption*. If declarer holds a different hand, and the contract is unbeatable, shrug it off and go on to the next deal. But don't let declarer make his contract when you have a way to defeat him.

QUIZ ON COUNTING DEFENSIVE TRICKS AND DEFENDING ON AN ASSUMPTION

1.

```
              ♠ A K 8 6
              ♡ 8 6
              ◇ Q 8 5
              ♣ A K Q J
   ♠ Q 10 5
   ♡ J 9 7 5 2        N
   ◇ K 7 3          W   E
   ♣ 10 7             S
```

North opened 1♣, South responded 1♠, North raised to 4♠. You lead the ♡5. Partner plays the king, and declarer wins the ace. Declarer cashes the ♠A and ♠K, partner following once, and then begins to run dummy's clubs. How do you defend?

6

2.

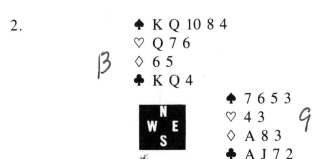

♠ K Q 10 8 4
♥ Q 7 6
♦ 6 5
♣ K Q 4

B

♠ 7 6 5 3
♥ 4 3   *9*
♦ A 8 3
♣ A J 7 2

South opened 1 ♥ , North responded 1 ♠ . South rebid 2 ♥ , North raised to 4 ♥ . West leads the ♦ 2. How do you defend?

3.

♠ K 6
♥ A 7   *15*
♦ Q 10 8 7 6 3
♣ A 7 5

♠ 8 5 3
♥ 10 8 6 4 2   *5*
♦ K 4
♣ J 8 2

North opened 1 ♦ , South responded 2 NT, North raised to 3 NT. West leads the ♠ Q. Declarer takes dummy's king and leads a low diamond. How do you defend?

4.

♠ K 6
♥ A K 6   *17*
♦ K Q 10 4
♣ Q 7 6 5

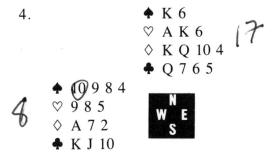

♠ 10 9 8 4
♥ 9 8 5
♦ A 7 2
♣ K J 10

4

North opened 1 NT, South responded 3 ♥ , North raised to 4 ♥ . You lead the ♠ 10. Dummy's king wins. Declarer plays the ace, king and queen of trumps, partner following twice with low cards. Declarer then tables the ◊ J. How do you defend?

5.

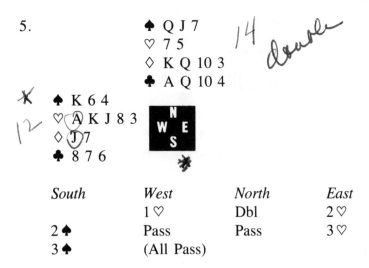

	♠ Q J 7
	♡ 7 5
	◊ K Q 10 3
	♣ A Q 10 4

♠ K 6 4
♡ A K J 8 3
◊ J 7
♣ 8 7 6

South	West	North	East
	1 ♡	Dbl	2 ♡
2 ♠	Pass	Pass	3 ♡
3 ♠	(All Pass)		

You lead the ♡ A and continue with the ♡ K. Declarer follows low to both tricks. How do you continue?

6.

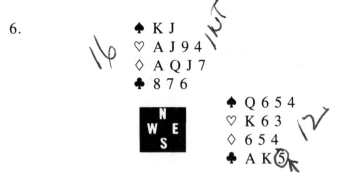

♠ K J	♠ Q 6 5 4
♡ A J 9 4	♡ K 6 3
◊ A Q J 7	◊ 6 5 4
♣ 8 7 6	♣ A K 5

North opened 1 NT, South responded 3 ♡, North raised to 4 ♡. West leads the ♠ 10. You cover dummy's jack, and declarer wins the ace. At trick two declarer passes the ♡ Q to your king. How do you defend?

7.

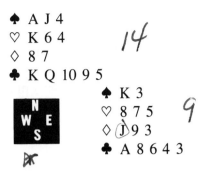

```
          ♠ A J 4
          ♡ K 6 4          14
          ◇ 8 7
          ♣ K Q 10 9 5
                        ♠ K 3
            N           ♡ 8 7 5       9
          W   E         ◇ J 9 3
            S           ♣ A 8 6 4 3
```

South opened 1 ♠, North responded 2 ♣. South rebid 2 NT, North tried 3 ♠, South bid 4 ♠. West leads the ♣2, and declarer follows low. How do you defend?

8.

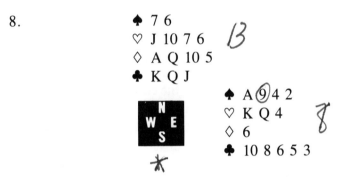

```
          ♠ 7 6
          ♡ J 10 7 6       13
          ◇ A Q 10 5
          ♣ K Q J
                        ♠ A 9 4 2
            N           ♡ K Q 4       7
          W   E         ◇ 6
            S           ♣ 10 8 6 5 3
```

South opened 1 ♡, North responded 3 ♡, South went on to 4 ♡. West leads the ♠K. How do you defend?

SOLUTIONS

1. West must ruff in on the third club and shift to diamonds (preferably by leading the king and another). Declarer is marked with the ♡Q from East's play of the king, so the defenders need three diamonds tricks. If West doesn't use his trump queen immediately, declarer will discard a diamond on the clubs.

2. Win the ◊A and shift to a *low* club. To take four tricks, you must find partner with either the ♠A or a trump trick — if he has neither, declarer will make five. Partner also needs the ♣10 (the 9 may do, if declarer misguesses); or, if partner has a high trump, any doubleton club. You hope to take the ◊A, partner's presumed trick, the ♣A, and either another club trick or a club ruff.

3. Play the ◊K, hoping to return a spade and establish partner's suit while he retains the ◊A as an entry. If declarer holds the ◊A, you won't beat the contract. Be an optimist!

4. Take the ◊A and lead your ♣K and ♣J. You must assume that partner has the ♣A. Perhaps you can take a diamond trick and three clubs.

5. To beat this contract, you must assume that partner has an ace. In that case, you can get a diamond ruff. Lead the ◊J at trick three. If declarer wins the ◊A and leads a trump toward dummy, you must jump in with your king and lead your other diamond. When partner wins the trump ace later, he returns a diamond, giving you a ruff with your last low trump. If partner's ace is in diamonds, he'll have to guess to duck the first round of diamonds, keeping communication with your hand.

6. Your only hope is to take three club tricks. Lead a *low* club from your A-K! If declarer has Q-10-x, he will probably play the 10, losing to partner's jack.

7. You can count three tricks: the ♣A, a club ruff and the ♠K. If partner has a red ace, the contract will be defeated easily. If he does not have an ace, however, he will need

the $\diamond$ K. In that case, you must lead a diamond at trick two, setting up partner's king while you still control trumps. The club ruff can wait, since you have a trump reentry. How do you know that partner has the $\diamond$ K? You don't, but that is the only time your play matters. You thus defend on the assumption that he holds the king.

8. You have two spade tricks and a trump trick. There will be no tricks in clubs or diamonds — declarer must have the ♣ A and $\diamond$ K for his opening bid — so the setting trick must come from trumps. Overtake the ♠ K and lead your singleton diamond. When declarer leads a trump from dummy, you *split your honors,* win the second trump and lead to partner's ♠ Q so he can give you a diamond ruff.

Lesson 2

BASIC IDEAS IN DEFENSIVE PLAY

The defenders must often rely on general principles for guidance as they play routinely to each trick (especially in the early play). The principles in this lesson guide defensive play in:

1. Choosing a card from the suit you lead.
2. Second-hand play, when declarer or dummy leads to the trick.
3. Covering honors.
4. Third-hand play, when your partner leads to the trick.
5. The Rule of Eleven.

1. Once you decide what suit to lead, the card you choose is often predetermined. Here are some guidelines.

> With a sequence (three or more cards adjacent in rank, of which the highest card is an honor) lead the *top* card in your sequence. Holdings such as K-Q-10-3 or Q-J-9-5-2, which contain two *equals* plus another nearly adjacent card, are treated as sequences — you still lead the top card.
>
> From broken suits, lead the *fourth-highest* card. However, if your suit is completely worthless, lead *highest* or *second-highest* to tell partner that your suit is weak.
>
> From a doubleton, lead the *top* card to get out of partner's way in case he has a strong holding.
>
> *Avoid underleading an ace against a suit contract.* Declarer may trump the next time the suit is led.
>
> Lead the *ace* from a suit headed by the A-K.
>
> In a suit partner bid, lead *low from length* if you have an honor. Lead high if you have only low cards.

2. The tendency in second-hand play is to *wait* by playing a low card. You don't need desperate tactics when your partner will get to play last. By adopting the strategy of playing low in second seat, you may:

Make declarer guess what to play from his hand or dummy in third seat.

Force declarer to spend a high card to keep your partner from winning the trick cheaply.

Avoid clashing your high cards with partner's.

Make it harder for declarer to set up his tricks.

Save your high cards to capture declarer's honors.

There are several exceptions in second-hand play. By playing high, you may:

Win a trick at no cost.

Stop declarer from winning an underserved trick.

Assure that you win at least one trick in a suit by *splitting your honors*.

Tell partner that you have a strong holding by playing the top card of a *sequence*.

3. Another exception to the tendency to play low in second seat occurs when declarer *leads an intermediate card*. Then you may want to *cover* with an intermediate of your own. By forcing declarer to spend two high cards on the same trick, you may promote your side's lower cards. For example:

```
              (Q) 6
8 7 3 2        ■               K 9 5
            A J 10 4
```

If declarer leads dummy's queen, East must cover with the

king to save a trick. Work out for yourself what happens if East fails to cover.

On some occasions you should refuse to *cover an honor*. Don't cover if:

> It's impossible to promote any tricks for your side by covering.
>
> You have an important honor (such as the well-guarded king of trumps) that declarer cannot capture.
>
> Declarer has a choice of ways to play the hand, and a cover will solve his problems.

It is seldom right to cover an honor if dummy leads from a solid holding (such as Q-J-10-9-4). If dummy holds a *broken* sequence, however, such as Q-J-4 or J-10-6, it's usually correct to cover the *last* honor in the sequence.

Remember, cover an honor *only* if you see a chance to promote intermediate cards for your side.

4. The tendency by third hand is to play *high*. The goal is the same as in covering honors — the prospect of *promoting* the defenders' intermediate cards. By playing a high card in third seat, you make declarer pay to win the trick. Be willing to sacrifice a high card to promote lesser cards in your hand or partner's hand.

Third hand high has many exceptions. If you cannot gain by sacrificing a high card in third position, you aren't obligated to play it. Also, it may be correct to finesse against dummy as third hand, such as in this position:

♠ Q 6 5

■   ♠ K 10 4

West leads the ♠2 against a heart contract. East knows that declarer holds the ♠A, since West wouldn't underlead an ace against a suit contract. If dummy plays low, East should play the *10*, hoping it will force declarer's ace.

As third hand to play from a sequence, play the *lowest* card. This strategy gives partner maximum information about your holding.

5. The *Rule of Eleven* is a device the defenders use to make judgments in third-hand play.

> *Assuming that partner's lead is fourth highest, subtract his spot from 11. The remainder gives the number of higher-ranking cards that lie in your hand and the opponents' hands.*

♣ K 5 3̶

■   ♣ A J 9 2   *where is the Q ?*

West leads the ♣7 against a notrump contract, and dummy plays *low*. You can apply the Rule of Eleven. Subtract seven (your partner's spot) from 11. The remainder, four, is the number of cards higher than the seven held by dummy, you and declarer. Since you can see all four of these cards, you know declarer cannot beat the 7. You therefore play your 2, letting partner win so he can lead through dummy's ♣K again.

The ideas in this lesson will serve you well. While you shouldn't depart from them without a good reason, neither should you treat them as inviolable rules.

Review the material in this lesson. Then test your comprehension of basic ideas in defensive play.

I.   QUIZ ON CHOOSING A CARD TO LEAD

1. The opponents reach 4♠. Your side did not bid. You decide to lead a heart. Choose the proper card from these holdings.

1.	♡ K Q J 5	16.	♡ A J 8 6 4
2.	♡ Q J 10 4	17.	♡ A 7
3.	♡ J 10 9 6 4	18.	♡ Q 7
4.	♡ K Q 10 5	19.	♡ J 10 5
5.	♡ Q J 9 6 3	20.	♡ J 6
6.	♡ Q 10 8 6 4	21.	♡ 9 5
7.	♡ J 9 6 4	22.	♡ 9 8 7
8.	♡ Q J 7 6	23.	♡ 8 4 2
9.	♡ K Q 4 2	24.	♡ A K 7 5 3 *only 2 cards*
10.	♡ Q J 7	25.	♡ A K *K 7 A*
11.	♡ K 10 9 8 4	26.	♡ 10 9 8 5 3
12.	♡ A 8 5 4 2	27.	♡ A Q J 9 6

13. ♡ Q 10 9 6 4   28. ♡ Q 9 8 7 4
14. ♡ K J 10 6   29. ♡ K Q
15. ♡ 9 8 7 4 2   30. ♡ J 10 7 2

2. The opponents reach 3 NT. Your side did not bid. You decide to lead a diamond. Choose the proper card from these holdings.

1. ◊ K Q J 5 4   9. ◊ A J 8 5 3
2. ◊ Q J 9 7 6   10. ◊ A 10 9 7 6 4
3. ◊ Q J 6 5 4   11. ◊ A Q J 9 5
4. ◊ J 9 7 6 4 2   12. ◊ 9 7 5
5. ◊ Q 10 9 7 4   13. ◊ 9 8 7 5 3
6. ◊ A J 10 8 5   14. ◊ 10 9 8 7 4
7. ◊ J 9 7 2   15. ◊ K J 10 8 6 3
8. ◊ Q 6   16. ◊ K 9 8 7 4

II. QUIZ ON SECOND-HAND PLAY

1. Dummy has ♠ 9 4 2. At some point, declarer leads a low spade from dummy. Choose the correct play from these holdings.

1. ♠ K J 6 3   6. ♠ Q 10 7 6
2. ♠ A 7 5   7. ♠ J 10 8 7 5
3. ♠ K Q J 7   8. ♠ A Q J 10
4. ♠ A J 3   9. ♠ Q J 5
5. ♠ A K 7 5 3   10. ♠ K Q 6 5

2. Dummy leads low from K-7-5. You are to play in second seat from A-J-4. Which card is usually correct?

3. Declarer is playing notrump and leads low from dummy's A-8-5. You are next to play from K-10-7-3. Which card do you play?

4. Dummy leads low from K-7-5. You are to play next with Q-J-6. Which card do you play?

18

5.　Declarer is playing notrump and leads low from his hand toward dummy's J-6. You are next to play from A-Q-9-④. Which card is usually correct?

6.　Declarer is playing a heart contract and leads a spade from his hand toward dummy's Q-5. You are next to play from Ⓚ-J-9-7. Which card do you play?

III. QUIZ ON COVERING HONORS

In these situations, decide whether you would *cover* the honor led by declarer.

to get (1) trick

1. Ⓠ 6 ▪	Ⓚ 9 8 5	Dummy leads the queen at notrump.
2. Ⓙ 7 ▪	Ⓠ 4	Dummy leads the jack at notrump. *Cover*
3. ⑩ Q 8 *J*	A Ⓚ J 7 6 ▪	Declarer leads the 10 at notrump.
4. Q 6 5	A 10 9 ⑧ ▪	Declarer leads the jack at notrump.
5. Ⓠ J 10 8 6 ▪	K 7 5 ③	Dummy leads the queen at notrump.
6. Ⓙ 6 ▪	Ⓐ 4	Dummy leads the jack at notrump. *Cover*
7. Ⓠ 6 ▪	K 5 4 ③	This suit is trumps. Declarer leads the queen from dummy. *not sure where "A" is.—*
8. Ⓙ 7 ▪	Q 6 ⑤	This suit is trumps, declarer having bid and rebid the suit. Declarer leads the jack from dummy.

19

9. J 10 4

Q 7 6

Dummy leads the jack at notrump.

10. 10 9 7

J 8 6

Dummy leads the 10 at no-trump.

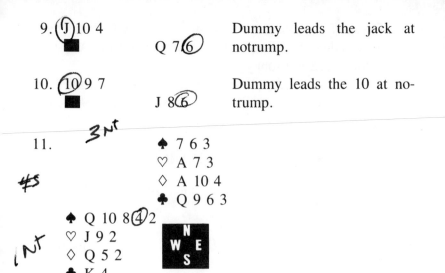

11. 3NT

♠ 7 6 3
♡ A 7 3
◇ A 10 4
♣ Q 9 6 3

♠ Q 10 8 4 2
♡ J 9 2
◇ Q 5 2
♣ K 4

```
   N
W     E
   S
```

South opened 1 NT, North raised to 3 NT. You lead the ♠4 to partner's jack and declarer's king. At trick two declarer leads the ◇J. Do you cover?

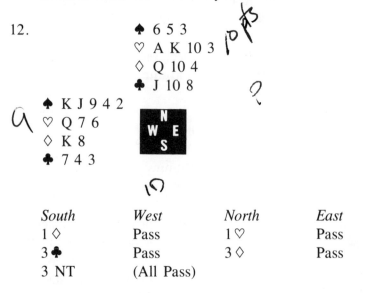

12.

♠ 6 5 3
♡ A K 10 3
◇ Q 10 4
♣ J 10 8

♠ K J 9 4 2
♡ Q 7 6
◇ K 8
♣ 7 4 3

```
   N
W     E
   S
```

South	West	North	East
1 ◇	Pass	1 ♡	Pass
3 ♣	Pass	3 ◇	Pass
3 NT	(All Pass)		

You lead the ♠4. Partner produces the queen, and declarer wins the ace. Next, declarer tables the ♡J. Do you cover?

IV. QUIZ ON THIRD-HAND PLAY

In these situations, declarer is playing 4 ♠, and your partner leads the ♡2. When dummy plays low, what do you play in third seat?

1. ♡ 7 6 4
   ■   ♡ K 9 5

2. ♡ Q J 9 8
   ■   ♡ K 7 5 4

3. ♡ Q 6 5
   ■   ♡ K 10 4 3

4. ♡ A 10 7
   ■   ♡ Q 9 6 4

5. ♡ Q 7 6
   ■   ♡ K 9 5

6. ♡ J 7 3
   ■   ♡ Q 9 6

7. ♡ 7 6 5
   ■   ♡ J 10 9

8. ♡ 7 6 5
   ■   ♡ K Q 8 4

9. ♡ 8 4 3
   ■   ♡ Q J 10 6

10. ♡ 6 5 4
    ■   ♡ Q J 8 3

11. ♡ J 8 6
    ■   ♡ K 10 9 5

12. ♡ 8 6 4
    ■   ♡ A J 7

13. You led the ◇4 from K-10-8-4-3 against a 3 NT contract. Dummy has 9-2 and plays low. Your partner plays the queen, and declarer wins the ace. Who has the ◇J?

14. You lead the ♠4 from J-9-7-4 against a 4♡ contract. Dummy has 6-5-3 and plays low, your partner plays the king and declarer wins the ace. Who has the ♠Q?

QUIZ ON THE RULE OF ELEVEN

1. ♠ Q 9 4 3
   ♠ K J 6

West leads the ♠ 5 against a 4 ♡ contract. Dummy plays low. Which spade do you play?

2. ♠ J 8 6
   ♠ K 9 4

West leads the ♠ 5 against 4 ♡. Dummy plays low. Which spade do you play?

3.
♠ Q 8 6 4
♡ Q 8 6 4
◇ A J 7
♣ 6 5

	N	
W		E
	S	

♠ 7 5
♡ K J 7
◇ K 9 3
♣ J 8 7 4 3

South opened 1 ♠, North raised to 2 ♠, South jumped to 4 ♠. West leads the ◇ 6, and dummy plays the 7. What do you play as East?

SOLUTIONS TO QUIZ ON CHOOSING A CARD TO LEAD

1.
1. K
2. Q
3. J
4. K
5. Q
6. 6
7. 4
8. 6
9. K (to assure *one* trick)
10. Q (from three cards, lead the queen even though you don't have a true sequence)
11. 10
12. A
13. 10
14. J
15. 9
16. A
17. A
18. Q
19. J
20. J
21. 9
22. 9
23. 8
24. A
25. K (from A-K *alone*)
26. 10
27. A
28. 7 → why not 9?
29. K
30. 2

2.
1. K
2. Q
3. 5
4. 6
5. 10
6. J
7. 2
8. Q
9. 5
10. 10
11. Q
12. 9
13. 9
14. 10
15. J
16. 7

SOLUTIONS TO QUIZ ON SECOND-HAND PLAY

1.
1. 3
2. 5
3. K,   suggesting a sequence.

    4. 3

    5. K,   but it could be right to duck, giving declarer a guess if he has Q-10-x.

    6. 6

    7. J,   suggesting a sequence.

    8. A,   best in most cases.

    9. 5

    10. 5,   unless you need to assure *one* trick, in which case play the king.

2.   Play the *4*. Perhaps you will take tricks with both your ace *and* jack.

3.   Play *low*. In many positions you give away a trick if you jump up with the king. It usually pays to stick with *second hand low*.

4.   Play the *queen,* to assure one trick.

5.   Play *low*. You prefer to capture one of declarer's high cards with your honors.

6.   Play the king to win the trick. To win cannot cost, and you may never get your king if you don't take it now.

SOLUTIONS TO QUIZ ON COVERING HONORS

1.   Cover, with your good intermediate cards. You can assure at least one trick.

2.   Cover.

3.   Cover. Perhaps partner has 9-x-x-x.

4.   Don't cover. Dummy has all the intermediates, so to cover gains nothing.

5.   Don't cover. You can see all the intermediates in dummy.

6.   Cover.

7.   Don't cover. Protect your king as a sure trick.

8.   Don't cover. If declarer has great length, you have no intermediates to promote.

9.   Don't cover, but cover if dummy leads the 10 later.

10.   Don't cover, but cover if dummy leads the 9 later.

11. Don't cover. Declarer is probably trying to set up his best suit, so you will probably help *him* if you cover.

12. Declarer has all the missing high cards for his jump to 3 ♣, so he has one spade trick, two hearts, one diamond, and (you hope) no more than four clubs. If you duck the ♡ J, he must guess which red-suit finesse to take for his contract. If you cover, he has nine tricks. Note that you must be ready to duck *without a giveaway pause.* You give away the location of the ♡ Q if you hesitate when declarer leads the ♡ J.

SOLUTIONS TO QUIZ ON THIRD-HAND PLAY

1. K   8. Q
2. 4   9. 10
3. 10   10. J
4. 9   11. 9
5. 9   12. A
6. 9   13. Declarer. Partner would play the jack
7. 9   in third seat from Q J
          14. Declarer. Partner would play the queen in third
                seat from K Q.

SOLUTIONS TO QUIZ ON THE RULE OF ELEVEN

1. Play the 6. The Rule of Eleven tells you that declarer has only one spade higher than partner's 5, and it must be the ace.

2. Play the 9. Declarer has only one spade higher than partner's 5, and it must be the ace.

3. Play the ♢ 9. Declarer has no diamonds higher than partner's 6.

1.

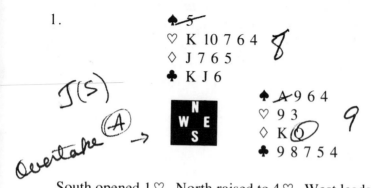

    ♠ 5
    ♡ K 10 7 6 4
    ◇ J 7 6 5
    ♣ K J 6

           ♠ A 9 6 4
           ♡ 9 3
           ◇ K Q
           ♣ 9 8 7 5 4

South opened 1 ♡ , North raised to 4 ♡ . West leads the ♠ J, and you win the ace. What do you lead at trick two?

2.

    ♠ 6 4 2
    ♡ 9 6 3
    ◇ A J 9 4
    ♣ J 7 3

♠ J 9 7 5 3
♡ K 10 5
◇ Q 10 5
♣ 9 6

South opened 1 ♣ , North responded 1 ◇ , South jumped to 3 NT. Your spade lead goes to the 6, queen and king. Declarer then leads a low diamond toward dummy. Plan your defense.

3.

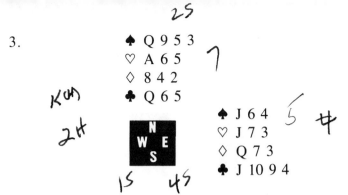

                ♠ Q 9 5 3
                ♡ A 6 5
                ◇ 8 4 2
                ♣ Q 6 5
                              ♠ J 6 4
                              ♡ J 7 3
                              ◇ Q 7 3
                              ♣ J 10 9 4

South opened 1♠; West overcalled 2♡. North raised to
2♠, South jumped to 4♠. West leads the ♡K. Declarer ducks
and wins the second heart with dummy's ace. He ruffs a heart,
draws three rounds of trumps, and plays the ♣A and ♣K and
a club to dummy's queen. Now declarer leads a low diamond
from dummy. What card do you play and why?

4.

                ♠ 7 6
                ♡ A 6 5
                ◇ K Q 10 5 4
                ♣ Q 8 7
                              ♠ A Q 5
                              ♡ 9 8 7 4
                              ◇ A 3 2
                              ♣ J 9 3

South opened 1 NT, North raised to 3 NT. West leads the
♠4. Plan your defense.

5.

♠ 7 5
♡ 9 6 5
◇ K Q J 10
♣ A J 6 5

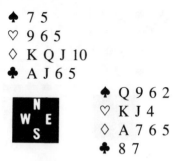

♠ Q 9 6 2
♡ K J 4
◇ A 7 6 5
♣ 8 7

South opened 1♣, North responded 1◇; South rebid 2♣, North raised to 3♣; South jumped to 5♣. West leads the ♡2. Plan your defense.

6.

♠ 9 4
♡ A 6 5
◇ K 7 6 5
♣ K 7 6 5

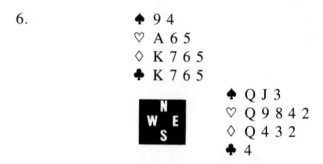

♠ Q J 3
♡ Q 9 8 4 2
◇ Q 4 3 2
♣ 4

South opened 1 NT, North raised to 3 NT. West leads the ♠7. Your jack is won by declarer's king. Declarer leads a club to dummy's king and a club back toward his hand. What do you discard on this trick?

7.

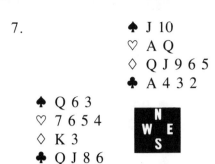

♠ J 10
♡ A Q
◇ Q J 9 6 5
♣ A 4 3 2

♠ Q 6 3
♡ 7 6 5 4
◇ K 3
♣ Q J 8 6

North opened 1 ◇, South responded 1 ♡; North rebid 2 ♣, South tried 2 NT; North raised to 3 NT. You lead the ♠ 3. Partner wins the ace and returns the ♠ 7, won by declarer's king. How do you play to this trick?

8.

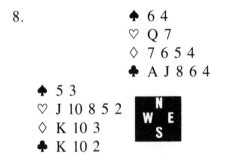

♠ 6 4
♡ Q 7
◇ 7 6 5 4
♣ A J 8 6 4

♠ 5 3
♡ J 10 8 5 2
◇ K 10 3
♣ K 10 2

East, your partner, opened 1 ♣. South jumped to 4 ♠ and everyone passed. You lead the ♡ J, covered by dummy's queen and partner's king. Declarer wins the ace and tables the ♣ Q. Do you cover?

9. Partner leads a spade vs. a 3 NT contract. You win the ace from A-8-4 and plan to return partner's suit. Which card you do lead?

10.

♠ A J 5 4
♡ 6
♦ A 8 7 6 5
♣ 9 7 4

♠ 9 8 7
♡ A J 10 9 5
♦ Q J 9
♣ 8 2

South	West	North	East
1 ♡	Pass	1 ♠	Pass
3 ♣	Pass	3 NT	Pass
4 ♣	Pass	6 ♣	(All Pass)

West leads the ♠K. Dummy wins the ace and leads a low heart. Plan your defense.

SOLUTIONS

1. Shift to the ♦Q. You must cash what diamond tricks you can. (If declarer holds the ♦A, you probably can't set him.) But if you lead the normal ♦K and follow with the queen, partner will play low with A-x-x-x, waiting for a third round. He should grasp the significance of your unusual diamond plays, overtake the king and give you a ruff.

2. Play the ♦Q, gaining a trick if declarer holds two or three low cards. You have nothing to lose by making this play — if declarer holds the ♦K, he is about to finesse dummy's jack successfully.

3. Put up the ♦Q to keep declarer from ducking the trick into partner's hand and endplaying him. To beat the contract, you must assume that partner's diamonds are A-J-10 or better.

𝒦 ᵠ

30

4. Play the ♠Q, forcing declarer to win if he has K-x-x and keeping communication with your partner's hand. You'll lead the ♠A and another spade when you win the ◇A, hoping partner started with J-x-x-x-x. If you win the ♠A at trick one, declarer can hold up his king effectively.

5. Play the ♡J as a *discovery* play. If declarer wins the ♡Q, you'll give up on hearts and switch to spades when you win the ◇A.

6. Discard the ♠Q. The Rule of Eleven indicates that the king was declarer's only spade higher than partner's 7, so all of partner's spades are now good. However, partner cannot know that — from his vantage point, declarer may have the ♠Q. You must discard the queen so partner will know he can cash his spades if he gets in (possibly with a club trick).

7. Partner's ♠7 must be his original fourth highest. (If he returned his original middle card from three, that would mean that declarer had five spades, which is impossible on the bidding.) In that case, the Rule of Eleven tells you that declarer has no card higher than partner's 7, and you can safely unblock your *queen*. When you win the ◇K, your side will take the rest of the spades.

8. Duck. Declarer's queen is probably a singleton. If you cover, you untangle the suit and let him discard a loser on dummy's ♣J.

9. Return the ♠8, your original middle card, from a three-card holding.

10. You should *duck* the heart lead. You won't lose your ace, since declarer can't ruff *all* his hearts in dummy. If declarer's hearts are K-Q-x-x-x, you gain by letting him win only *one* honor. If you put up your ace, he scores both the king and queen. One trick could be crucial on this deal.

Lesson 3

STRATEGY vs. NOTRUMP

You have three possible approaches to defense at notrump:

1. *ACTIVE*, the most common strategy, in which the defenders try to establish *long cards*. This is the fourth-from-the-longest-and-strongest approach — with the opening lead as an advantage, you lead your long suit at every opportunity, hoping to set up long cards before declarer has the tricks he needs. Long cards are usually the defenders' best chance, since declarer's side has more of the high cards.

   One problem implicit in this approach is that *the defender with the long suit must keep an entry to cash his winners.*

2. *PASSIVE,* indicated if declarer lacks a good source of tricks and may have trouble making his contract, especially if the defenders don't help him. In a passive defense, the defenders *exit safety* each time they must lead, trying not to give away tricks that aren't declarer's for the taking anyway.

3. *KILLING A SUIT.* If the defenders can deny declarer his best source of tricks, the contract often fails. In such cases, the defenders forget about setting up a suit of their own. Their strategy shifts to an attack on declarer's communication and entries.

QUIZ ON STRATEGY vs. NOTRUMP

1.

♠ A K 2
♡ K 10 2
◇ J 3
♣ Q J 10 8 4

15   1C   3NT

9D

N W E S

♠ J 4 3
♡ Q 4 3
◇ A K 8 7 4 2
♣ 2

10   1D

10   2NT

You are defending 3 NT. North opened 1 ♣, you overcalled 1 ◇, South bid 2 NT, North raised to 3 NT. Partner leads the ◇ 9. Plan your defense.

3 UT

2.

♠ 8 4
♡ 8 6 4
◇ K Q 10 5 4 3
♣ A 2

3S

N W E S

♠ 10 9 2
♡ J 9 5 3
◇ A J 2
♣ J 8 6

1 NT

You defend 3 NT. South opened 1 NT, and North raised to game. Partner leads the ♠ 3, and declarer wins your 9 with the jack. Next, declarer leads a diamond to dummy's queen. How do you defend?

*LET'S SEE . . . SHOULD I BE
PASSIVE OR ACTIVE
ON THIS HAND?*

3.

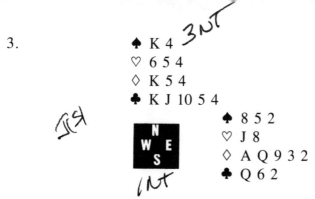

        ♠ K 4
        ♡ 6 5 4
        ♢ K 5 4
        ♣ K J 10 5 4

                ♠ 8 5 2
                ♡ J 8
                ♢ A Q 9 3 2
                ♣ Q 6 2

You defend 3 NT. South opened 1 NT, and North raised to game. Partner leads the ♠ J. Declarer wins dummy's king, leads a heart to his ace and passes the ♣ 9 to your queen. Plan your defense.

4.

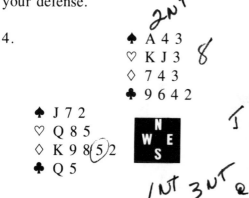

        ♠ A 4 3
        ♡ K J 3
        ♢ 7 4 3
        ♣ 9 6 4 2

♠ J 7 2
♡ Q 8 5
♢ K 9 8 5 2
♣ Q 5

You defend 3 NT. South opened 1 NT, North raised to 2 NT, South went on to game. You lead the ♢ 5, which goes to partner's jack and declarer's queen. Declarer then leads a heart to the king and a heart back to the 10. You win the queen. How do you defend?

35

5.
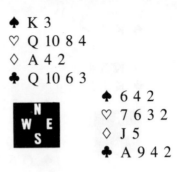

♠ K 3
♡ Q 10 8 4
◇ A 4 2
♣ Q 10 6 3

♠ 6 4 2
♡ 7 6 3 2
◇ J 5
♣ A 9 4 2

You defend 3 NT. South opened 1 NT, and North raised to game. Partner leads the ♠ Q. Declarer wins in dummy with the king and leads a low club. How do you defend?

6.

♠ 7 5 3
♡ J 8 3
◇ K 10 9 8 5 3
♣ A

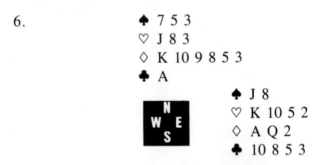

♠ J 8
♡ K 10 5 2
◇ A Q 2
♣ 10 8 5 3

You defend 3 NT. South opened 1 NT, and North raised to game. Partner leads the ♠ 2, and declarer takes your jack with the king. Declarer then leads the ◇ J, playing low from dummy. You duck, and declarer continues with another diamond, partner discarding. After winning the queen on the second diamond, how do you continue?

SOLUTIONS

1. Duck the first trick. To play the ace, king and another diamond won't help because you have no entry to your long cards. You must keep the partnership communication open. Maybe partner will win a trick with the ♣A or ♣K and will have another diamond to lead. Then you can run your suit.

2. Duck the first diamond. If declarer has two diamonds, this play prevents him from setting up the suit. You retain a *double* stopper while declarer has only one diamond left in his hand. Killing declarer's long suit should be your goal, especially when partner is known to have only four spades.

3. Return a low diamond. Partner is marked with the ♣A, since declarer did not cash that card before finessing for the queen. In that case, partner's spades cannot be as good as A-J-10-x-x — declarer must have the ace as well as the queen. Try to beat the contract with diamond tricks instead of returning partner's lead.

4. *Exit safely* with a heart. With dummy so weak, and with any other return likely to cost a (perhaps crucial) trick, it's time to go passive.

5. Hop up with the ♣A to return partner's suit. You spend your entry early, trying to set up the spades while partner saves his entries.

6. Shift to a club, knocking out declarer's only entry to the diamond suit. Without diamond tricks, his chances of making the contract are slim.

Lesson 4

STRATEGY vs. SUIT CONTRACTS

You have several possible approaches to the defense at a suit contract. Your choice depends on the strengths and weaknesses of dummy.

1. ACTIVE. This approach is indicated when dummy (rarely, declarer's own hand) has a strong side suit that will provide discards for declarer's losers. The defenders must therefore win tricks *quickly*. They cash aces and lead from kings and queens in a desperate try to establish and cash fast tricks.

2. PASSIVE. This approach is indicated when dummy has little trick-taking power and declarer will have trouble avoiding losers. The defenders want to *exit safely* each time they must lead, trying not to give away tricks that aren't declarer's for the taking anyway.

3. LEADING TRUMPS. This approach is indicated if dummy's only source of tricks is ruffing power (or if a crossruff is likely). The defenders must keep declarer from winning extra tricks by scoring his trumps separately.

4. FORCING. In this approach the defenders make declarer ruff so many times that he runs out of trumps, loses control of the play and cannot use his side suits. A forcing defense is most attractive when a defender holds unexpected length in trumps (four or more) and a long suit to lead.

5. TRYING FOR RUFFS. Leading a singleton or doubleton to try for a ruff is most attractive when you have a *weak hand* (partner is likely to have entries)

and when you have the ace or king of trumps for a *sure reentry*. Avoid this approach when you have (1) a strong hand, (2) natural trump tricks, or (3) long, weak trumps.

6. EXTRA TRUMP TRICKS. In an *uppercut*, a defender ruffs with an intermediate trump, forcing declarer to weaken his trump holding by overruffing. In a *trump promotion*, declarer is in a dilemma — he must ruff low and be overruffed or ruff high and fatally weaken his trump holding.

Taking extra trump tricks may be the only chance for the defense, but the uppercut and the trump promotion work best *after* the defenders have taken all their side-suit tricks. Otherwise, declarer may counter effectively by discarding a loser instead of ruffing.

Note well: A common error is the failure to understand the active-passive concept in defense. The most important attribute of a good defender is the ability to distinguish the tricks he must take quickly from the tricks that can wait.

*A TRUMP PROMOTION MAY BE THE ONLY WAY
TO DEFEAT THE CONTRACT.*

QUIZ ON STRATEGY vs. SUIT CONTRACTS

1.
                    ♠ K 10 3 2
                    ♡ A 7 5
                    ◇ Q 8 4
                    ♣ A J 3

    ♠ Q 7 5
    ♡ K Q J 2
    ◇ K 9 3
    ♣ 8 6 4

You are defending 2 ♠. North opened 1 ♣, South bid 1 ♠,
North raised. Declarer wins your ♡ K with the ace and leads
the ♠ K and a spade to the jack. You win the queen and cash
the ♡ Q and ♡ J, all following. How do you continue?

2.
          ♠ A Q
          ♡ J 9 6 4
          ◇ A J 3
          ♣ K 7 5 2

♠ 8 4
♡ K Q 5
◇ K 10 5 2
♣ Q J 10 8

You defend 4 ♡. Dummy opened 1 NT, declarer responded 3 ♠ and converted 3 NT to 4 ♡. Your ♣ Q holds the first trick, but declarer ruffs the next club. He leads a spade to the ace and finesses the ♡ J to your queen. What do you lead?

3.
          ♠ A K 2
          ♡ 10 9 8
          ◇ 10 6 2
          ♣ Q 10 8 7

♠ 4 3
♡ A 7 6 5
◇ K J 9 7 5
♣ 6 5

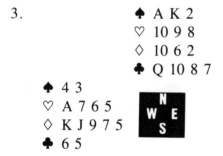

You defend 4 ♡. Declarer opened 1 ♡, dummy raised and declarer went on to game. You lead a diamond to partner's ace. He cashes the ◇ Q and leads a third diamond, ruffed by declarer. Declarer now leads the ♡ K. How do you defend?

4.

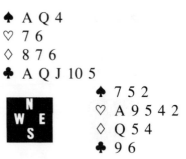

♠ A Q 4
♡ 7 6
◇ 8 7 6
♣ A Q J 10 5

♠ 7 5 2
♡ A 9 5 4 2
◇ Q 5 4
♣ 9 6

You defend 4♠. Declarer opened 1♠, dummy responded 2♣ and raised declarer's 2♠ rebid to game. Partner leads the ♡Q. How do you defend?

5.

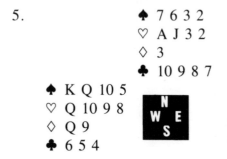

♠ 7 6 3 2
♡ A J 3 2
◇ 3
♣ 10 9 8 7

♠ K Q 10 5
♡ Q 10 9 8
◇ Q 9
♣ 6 5 4

You defend 2♣. Declarer opened 1◇, dummy responded 1♡ and passed declarer's 2♣ rebid. Your ♠K holds the first trick, partner playing the 9 and declarer the jack. What do you do now?

6.
       ♠ A K 3
       ♡ 3
       ◇ J 7 6 5
       ♣ A Q 6 5 4
♠ 6 5 4
♡ A 9 2
◇ 9 8
♣ 10 8 7 3 2

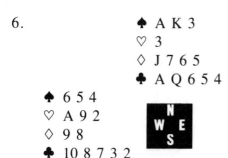

You defend 4♡. Your partner opened 1◇, and declarer preempted with 4♡. Partner overtakes your ◇9 lead with the 10 and cashes the queen. On the ◇K, declarer ruffs with the ♡K. How do you defend?

7.
       ♠ 9 5 4
       ♡ J 8 6
       ◇ A K Q 10 4
       ♣ Q 7
♠ A K 10 6 3
♡ 9 5 2
◇ J 9
♣ K 8 2

You defend 4♡. Declarer opened 1♡, you overcalled 1♠. Dummy bid 2◇ and raised declarer's 2♡ rebid to game. You cash the ♠A and ♠K, declarer following with the jack and queen. What do you lead at trick three?

8. You, West, hold:

♠ A Q 7 5 3
♡ A K 5
♢ 10 9 7 4
♣ 2

South	West	North	East
1 ♡	1 ♠	2 ♣	Pass
3 ♣	Pass	3 ♡	Pass
4 ♡	(All Pass)		

What is your opening lead?

SOLUTIONS

1. Go *passive* by returning your last trump. With dummy so weak, your minor-suit tricks aren't going anywhere. Let declarer break the minor suits.

2. Get *active* with a diamond return, hoping to set up a trick if partner has the queen. If you don't lead a diamond now, declarer will have time to draw trumps and discard dummy's diamonds on his spades. If he has a losing diamond, he will then ruff it in dummy.

3. Hold up your ace of trumps until dummy has none left. Then you can force declarer to ruff another diamond lead *in his hand*. If he started with only five trumps, he will lose control — you will have a long trump and a good diamond. If declarer stops playing trumps after seeing the 4-1 split, he can keep control by cashing his black-suit winners and forcing *you* to ruff with your low trump. Nevertheless, you get four tricks.

4. Win the ♡A and shift to the ♢Q. You need three *fast* diamond tricks to beat the contract, and partner must therefore hold A-J-10. If you lead a low diamond instead,

declarer will play low, ducking the trick safely to partner and losing only two diamonds.

5. Shift to trumps to cut down on dummy's only source of tricks. (You also keep declarer from ruffing spades in his hand.)

6. You should *discard* on the third diamond. If partner has a trump as high as the 10, your A-9-2 will then be worth *two* tricks. If you overruff the ♡K with your ace, you are letting declarer force out your ace with his king, which he intended to do anyway. It is seldom right to overruff with a natural trump winner. Let your trumps increase in value.

7. Shift to a club, hoping declarer's hand is something like:

♠ Q J
♡ A K Q x x x
♢ x x
♣ J x x

You can't beat the contract if declarer holds the ♣A.

8. Lead the ♢10. Avoid leading your club singleton, since the contract will always be defeated if partner has the ♣A. If, as is far more likely, he has the ♣Q or ♣J, a club lead will help declarer.

*YOU HAVE MANY CHOICES AVAILABLE
WHEN YOU'RE THE OPENING LEADER.*

Lesson 5

EDUCATED GUESSING ON OPENING LEAD

In choosing an opening lead:

REMEMBER your available defensive strategies. The opening lead is the first step in adopting a strategy.

LISTEN to the bidding. Anticipate what source of tricks dummy will provide.

VISUALIZE dummy and imagine how the play will go. How will declarer try to make his contract? Does any feature of your hand indicate whether declarer will succeed in his probable line of play? Apply the right defensive strategy, *beginning with the opening lead*, to counter declarer's plans.

Against suit contracts:

If your strategy is:	Your opening lead will be:
ACTIVE	AGGRESSIVE. Lead from honors or lay down aces.
PASSIVE	SAFE. Lead trumps or lead from a sequence.
PREVENTING RUFFS	A TRUMP, drawing two of declarer's trumps for one of yours.
THE FORCING GAME	YOUR LONGEST SUIT.
TRYING FOR RUFFS	FROM SHORTNESS. Rarely, you will lead a suit *partner* may be short in.
EXTRA TRUMP TRICKS FROM SHORTNESS OR LENGTH.	A short-suit lead may result in a trump promotion; a long-suit lead may result in an uppercut.

Against notrump contracts:

If your strategy is:	Your opening lead will be:
ACTIVE	YOUR LONGEST SUIT or partner's long suit.
PASSIVE	SAFE. Lead through dummy's bid suit or lead from a sequence.
KILLING A SUIT	The suit that contains an entry to declarer's (or dummy's) long suit.

QUIZ ON OPENING LEADS

1. ♠ x x   *LHO*   *RHO*
   ♡ K J 9 x x   1♡   1♠
   ◇ A x   2♡   3♠
   ♣ Q J 9 x   4♠   Pass

2. ♠ A x x x   *LHO*   *RHO*
   ♡ x   1♣
   ◇ K Q 10 x x   1♡   1♠
   ♣ Q x x   3♠   4♠
              Pass

3. ♠ 10 x   *LHO*   *RHO*
   ♡ Q x x   1♠
   ◇ J 10 9 x   2♡   2♠
   ♣ K 10 8 x   3♠   4♠
              Pass

4. ♠ 9 x   *LHO*   *RHO*
   ♡ K x x   1 NT
   ◇ J x x x   2♣   2♡
   ♣ 10 9 8 x   4♡   Pass

5. ♠ K J 9 x   *LHO*   *RHO*
   ♡ A x   1♠
   ◇ x x x x   1 NT   2◇
   ♣ Q 9 x   Pass

6. ♠ x x   *LHO*   *RHO*
   ♡ Q 10 x x   1♠
   ◇ K J x x   2♣   2♡
   ♣ J x x   2♠   3♠
              4♠   Pass

7. ♠ 10 x   LHO   RHO
    ♡ Q 10 x x x   1 ◊   1 ♡
    ◊ x x x x   2 ◊   3 NT
    ♣ 10 x

8. ♠ A 10 9 x   LHO   RHO
    ♡ x   1 ♠
    ◊ Q J 10 x   2 ♡   2 ♠
    ♣ J x x x   3 ♠   Pass

9. ♠ K Q x x   You   LHO   Partner   RHO
    ♡ x   1 ♡
    ◊ K J x x x   Dbl   Pass Pass   Pass
    ♣ A J x

10. ♠ Q J x x   LHO   RHO
    ♡ x x   1 ♠   2 ♣
    ◊ A Q 10 x   2 ♡   2 NT
    ♣ x x x   3 ♣   4 ♣
                    5 ♣   Pass

11. ♠ x x   LHO   RHO
    ♡ J 10 9 x   1 ◊   1 ♠
    ◊ Q J 10 x   2 ♠   Pass
    ♣ K x x

12. ♠ J 10 x   You   LHO   Partner   RHO
    ♡ K 10 x   1 ♠   2 ♣
    ◊ K 9 x x   2 ♠   3 ♣   4 ♠   5 ♣
    ♣ x x x   Dbl   Pass Pass   Pass

13. ♠ 10 x x   You   LHO   Partner   RHO
    ♡ x x   1 ♣   1 ♠   2 ♡
    ◊ Q J x x   Pass 3 ♡   Pass   3 NT
    ♣ K J 9 x   Pass 4 ♡   Pass   Pass
                    Pass

49

14. ♠ K x x x x
    ♡ Q x
    ♢ x x x
    ♣ x x x

You	LHO	Partner	RHO
		1♠	Pass
2♠	Dbl	3♠	4♡
Pass	Pass	Pass	

15. ♠ K 10 x
    ♡ K 10 x x
    ♢ x
    ♣ x x x x x

LHO	RHO
1♢	1♡
3♢	3♡
3♠	3 NT
Pass	

16. ♠ J x x x
    ♡ 10 x
    ♢ Q 10 x x
    ♣ K x x

LHO	RHO
	1♢
1♡	1 NT
2 NT	Pass

17. ♠ A K 9 5 2
    ♡ x x x
    ♢ Q x
    ♣ A x x

LHO	RHO
	1 NT
3 NT	Pass

SOLUTIONS

1. ♣Q. Go passive, since you have dummy's long suit under control. You need not lay down the ◇A — declarer can't throw diamonds on dummy's hearts. Partner is unlikely to have the ◇K anyway, on the bidding.

2. ◇K. Try for a forcing game with your four trumps.

3. Club. Get active. Dummy has a heart suit, and your ♡Q is poorly placed.

4. ♠9. Try for a ruff with a bad hand plus trump control.

5. Trump. Declarer will need spade ruffs in dummy.

6. Diamond. Although you have declarer's second suit under control, dummy has a side suit. Stopping heart ruffs in dummy is less important than getting your diamond trick(s) before declarer sets up the clubs for discards.

7. ♣10. Try to hit partner's suit, since declarer bid your suit and you have no entries. Partner is more likely to have clubs than spades. He is marked with a few points and he might have overcalled 1♠ with a decent suit. A 2♣ overcall, however, would have been riskier.

8. ◇Q. Leading your singleton is pointless when you have sure trump tricks anyway.

9. Trump. This is an odd variation on leading trumps. Partner must have a solid trump holding to convert your takeout double to penalty. If you lead trumps right away, you can stop declarer from winning tricks with low trumps.

10. Trump. The bidding marks dummy with diamond shortness, and declarer has diamond length. You don't have to fear that declarer will take tricks with dummy's spade suit.

11. ♡J. The normal, passive lead, with dummy known to have a minimum opening.

12. Trump. The opponents have sacrificed against your game. Since partner has a good hand, your side surely has most of the high-card strength. By leading trumps, you may stop declarer from ruffing losers, and there is no rush for you to do anything else.

13. Trump. Since you have good intermediates in clubs and diamonds, declarer's most likely source of extra tricks is spade ruffs in dummy. Dummy promised ruffing potential by converting 3 NT to hearts.

14. ♠K. Make an exception to the principle of leading low in partner's suit. If you *hold the first trick*, perhaps you can make an effective switch through dummy to partner's side strength.

15. ♠K. Imaginative. You hope to knock the ♠A out of dummy so declarer can't use it as a late entry to the diamonds.

16. ♡10. Passive. You have good diamonds, partner is marked with at least four hearts and the opponents have nothing extra in high cards.

17. ♠2. You have no reason to show count by leading fourth best, since partner will never win a trick. You may fool declarer, though. (For instance, he may think it's safe to knock out your ♣A.)

*MAKE SURE YOUR DEFENSIVE SIGNALS ARE
CLEAR TO PARTNER.*

Lesson 6

DEFENSIVE SIGNALS

In Lesson 2 you learned some ways the defenders can communicate despite the handicap of not seeing each other's hands. Another way of communication is the use of *defensive signals*. Three types of signals exist, and each one handles a common defensive problem. To avoid confusion, the signals have definite *priorities*.

I. ATTITUDE. Since the defenders' most common problem is what suit to lead (or whether to keep on leading a suit), this is the most important signal. A defender often signals attitude *as his partner leads* a suit; he can also show attitude in *discarding*.

> The play of a *high* spot is encouraging. The play of a *low* spot is discouraging and may, under some circumstances, demand a switch.

Some important things to remember about ATTITUDE signals:

1. The size of the spot cards is relative. A *4* may encourage if signaller holds A-K-4-3-2, an *8* may discourage if he has 10-9-8. In interpreting a signal, you must look at your own spots, declarer's and dummy's.
2. Decide what message you want to send, then play the *highest* or *lowest* spot you can afford. Avoid signalling with ambiguous spots that may confuse partner.
3. The purpose of a signal is not to announce or deny possession of certain cards, but to suggest a line of defense. Even if you are strong in the suit partner leads, you may signal low if you think it's better for him to lead a different suit.
4. Don't signal if the information may help declarer more than your partner.
5. In discarding, avoid signalling high with a card that may be a vital trick. Instead, discard low in your weaker suits.
6. In signalling from a sequence, play the *top* card, as though you were leading to the trick.
7. Although a high spot is usually a strong signal, a low spot may be ambiguous. It may demand a switch, if an attractive switch is clear; it may also be noncommittal, merely implying doubt or apathy about partner's suit.

II. COUNT. The defenders often want to signal *how many* cards they hold in a suit. Knowing the count may tell a defender exactly when to take a winner (thereby damaging declarer's communication) or help a defender count declarer's distribution.

The defenders usually show count only when *declarer* leads a suit. (When declarer voluntarily leads a suit, he usually has strength there. Showing attitude is no longer a concern — if the defenders signal at all, they shift to showing count.)

> The play of a *high* spot, often followed by a lower one, shows an *even* number of cards. The play of a *low* spot, perhaps followed by a higher one, shows an *odd* number of cards.

Some important things to remember about COUNT signals:

1. The attitude signal takes precedence over count. You may not signal count unless your attitude about a suit is known or obvious.
2. With rare exceptions, defenders use the count signal as *declarer* leads a suit.
3. Signal count only when it is *safe* (declarer, as well as partner, can see your signals!) and when partner *needs* the information.
4. You cannot signal your length exactly, only within a two-card range. In case of ambiguity, the bidding may provide a clue to declarer's exact length.
5. In signalling count, play the *highest* spot you can afford. Avoid ambiguous spots that may confuse partner.
6. To signal count in *trumps*, play *high-low* with an *odd* number. The *trump echo,* as it is called, often implies interest in ruffing.

III. SUIT PREFERENCE. This rare and beautiful signal is often overused and abused. The most important thing to remember about *suit preference* is that you need it *only in special situations*.

Whereas attitude and count signals give information about their own suit, suit-preference signals direct attention to a suit other than the one in which the signal is given.

In some cases, you can show strength in a *high-ranking suit* by playing an *unusually high card* in a different suit. You can show strength in a *low-ranking suit* by playing an *unusually low card* in a different suit.

Some important things to remember about SUIT-PREFERENCE signals:

1. The attitude and count signals take precedence over suit preference. Interpret partner's signal as suit preference *only* if he cannot conceivably want to signal attitude or count.
2. A typical suit-preference signal is an *unusual* play with an unmistakable significance.
3. Most of the time, the defenders can handle their signalling problems with attitude. Suit preference is reserved for special situations.
4. The suit-preference signal has many applications. You can indicate the location of an entry, tell partner what suit to lead next after you give him a ruff, or get him to switch to a *specific* suit when an attitude signal would make him guess which suit to switch to.

BE AN ETHICAL PLAYER! The card you play is *itself* a legitimate way to communicate with partner. However, it is unethical to convey information through gestures, remarks or deliberate hesitations. Some players signal encouragement by looking happy or thumping their card on the table when partner leads a suit they like; otherwise they scowl. Avoid these improper methods. Play bridge as a game of skill.

57

QUIZ ON DEFENSIVE SIGNALS

1.

♠ Q 7 6
♡ A Q 4 2
◇ 4 3 2
♣ 4 3 2

♠ 9 2
♡ J 7 5
◇ J 10 9 8
♣ J 10 9 8

South opened 1 ♡ ; West overcalled 1 ♠, North raised to 2 ♡ and all passed. West leads the ♠ A. What do you play? Suppose West continues with the ♠ K and ♠ 3, and you ruff. What do you lead?

2.

♠ 6 5 4
♡ 6 5 4
◇ 8 6
♣ Q J 9 7 4

♠ 7 2
♡ Q 10 8 7
◇ K 9 7 5
♣ A 8 3

South opened 2 NT, and all passed. West leads the ♠ J. What do you play? Suppose declarer wins the ♠ Q and leads the ♣ K. Partner plays the 6, and you duck. Declarer then continues with the ♣ 10. Partner follows with the 2, and declarer overtakes with dummy's jack. Do you win this trick or duck again?

3.
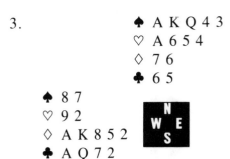

♠ A K Q 4 3
♡ A 6 5 4
◇ 7 6
♣ 6 5

♠ 8 7
♡ 9 2
◇ A K 8 5 2
♣ A Q 7 2

You opened 1 ◇ ; North overcalled 1 ♠ , East raised you to 2 ◇ and South bid 2 ♡ . North raised to 3 ♡ , South went on to 4 ♡ . You lead ◇ A. Partner plays the 10, declarer plays the 9. What do you lead next?

4.

♠ 7 6
♡ 9 5 3
◇ K Q 5 3 2
♣ A J 7

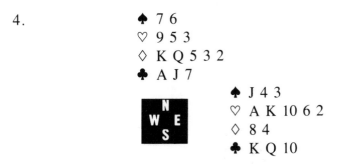

♠ J 4 3
♡ A K 10 6 2
◇ 8 4
♣ K Q 10

You opened 1 ♡ . South overcalled 2 ◇ , West raised you to 2 ♡ , North raised to 3 ◇ , passed out. West leads the ♡ Q. How do you signal?

5.

♠ 7 6 5
♡ K 5 3
◇ K 5 3
♣ Q J 10 4

♠ 8 2
♡ A Q 10 7 6
◇ 8 6 4
♣ 9 5 3

South opened 1 NT, North raised to 2 NT, South went on to 3 NT. West leads the ♠J. How do you play to this trick? Declarer wins the ♠Q and leads a low club to the queen. How do you play? Declarer now returns a club from dummy. How do you play?

6.

♠ 9
♡ K 10 4 3
◇ A K Q 8 6
♣ Q 9 4

♠ A K J 5 3
♡ A J 7 2
◇ 7 5 4
♣ 3

You opened 1♠; North doubled, East jumped to 3♠ (preemptive). South bid 4♣, North raised to 5♣. You lead the ♠A. Partner plays the 8, and declarer follows with the 4. How do you defend?

7.
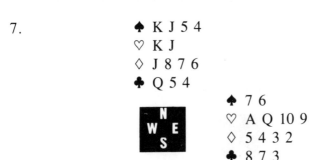

♠ K J 5 4
♡ K J
◇ J 8 7 6
♣ Q 5 4

♠ 7 6
♡ A Q 10 9
◇ 5 4 3 2
♣ 8 7 3

South opened 1 NT, North raised to 3 NT. West leads the ♠ 10. Declarer cashes the ♠ A and ♠ Q and leads a spade to dummy. What will you discard on the third and fourth spades?

8.
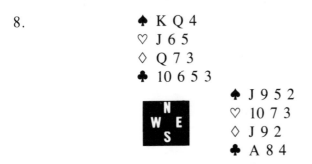

♠ K Q 4
♡ J 6 5
◇ Q 7 3
♣ 10 6 5 3

♠ J 9 5 2
♡ 10 7 3
◇ J 9 2
♣ A 8 4

West opened 1 ◇. You responded 1 ♠, South overcalled 2 ♣, North raised to 3 ♣, and everyone passed. West leads the ♠ A. How do you signal?

9.

♠ A 6 3
♡ J 10 4
◇ 7 6
♣ Q 9 7 6 4

♠ J 10 9 7 2
♡ 7 6
◇ J 5 3
♣ 10 8 3

West opened 1 ◇. The opponents took over and bid to 4 ♡. West leads the ♠ K, and dummy's ace wins. How do you signal?

10.
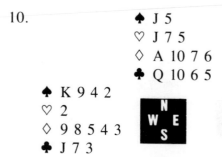

♠ J 5
♥ J 7 5
♦ A 10 7 6
♣ Q 10 6 5

♠ K 9 4 2
♥ 2
♦ 9 8 5 4 3
♣ J 7 3

South opened 1 ♣, North responded 2 ♣. East came in with 2 ♥. South and you passed, and North went to 3 ♣, passed out. You lead the ♥ 2. Your partner plays the queen, and South wins the ace. Declarer next tables the ♣ A. How do you play to this trick? Suppose declarer continues with a club to partner's king. Partner cashes the ♥ K and leads the ♥ 9, which you ruff. What do you lead now?

11.
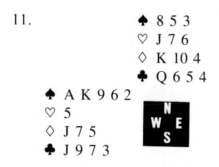

♠ 8 5 3
♥ J 7 6
♦ K 10 4
♣ Q 6 5 4

♠ A K 9 6 2
♥ 5
♦ J 7 5
♣ J 9 7 3

South opened 1 ♥, you overcalled 1 ♠. North raised to 2 ♥, and South invited with 3 ♥. This became the contract. You lead the ♠ A. Partner plays the 7, and declarer follows with the 4. How do you continue?

12.
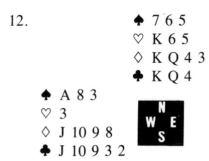

♠ 7 6 5
♥ K 6 5
♦ K Q 4 3
♣ K Q 4

♠ A 8 3
♥ 3
♦ J 10 9 8
♣ J 10 9 3 2

South opened 1 ♠, North responded 2 NT. South jumped to 4 NT (Blackwood), North responded 5 ♣, South signed off at 5 ♠. You lead the ♥3. Declarer takes partner's jack with the queen and leads the ♠K. How do you defend?

SOLUTIONS

1. Play the ♠9 at trick one (ATTITUDE), asking partner to continue spades, since you want to ruff. Partner's ♠3 (SUIT PREFERENCE) asks you to return clubs after taking your ruff.

2. Play the ♠2 (ATTITUDE) at trick one. On the second club lead, duck again. Partner's carding shows an even number of clubs (two, in this case), so declarer has another club.

3. Lead the ♦2. Partner's encouraging diamond should show the *queen*. (You know, from his raise, that he does not have a doubleton.) Your lead of the ♦2 (SUIT PREFERENCE) suggests a club return.

4. Signal with the ♥2, suggesting a *switch*. Partner will look at dummy and reason that a club is the most logical switch *from his side of the table*. Note that an attitude signal handles this deal nicely.

5. Play the ♠2 at trick one (ATTITUDE), showing a dislike for spades. Play the ♣3 at trick two (COUNT), showing an odd number. Play the ♣9 at trick three (SUIT

PREFERENCE), showing interest in hearts over diamonds.

6. Cash your ♡A and continue with ♠K. Partner's ♠8 is a routine ATTITUDE signal, asking you to continue spades. As it happens, he has K-6-5-2 of trumps and wants you to force dummy to ruff so his king will win a trick. Remember that a spade continuation is still a possible defense even if dummy can win the next trick.

7. Discard the ◇2 and the ♣3. By implication, you show interest in the suit you have not discarded. Note that if your diamonds were 10-4-3-2, you couldn't afford to discard one.

8. Play the ♠9 (ATTITUDE). True, you don't like partner's lead, but your signal should be based on the current situation. If you play a low spade, partner will think you want (or at least can stand) a shift. If he shifts to the ♡K from K-Q or lays down the ◇A, that could cost a critical trick.

9. Play the ♠J, signalling possession of the 10. If partner gets in (perhaps with a trump trick), he'll know how to give you the lead, and you can lead a diamond through declarer's holding.

10. Play your ♣7 on declarer's ace, starting an *echo* to show three trumps. Partner's ♡9 is SUIT PREFERENCE for spades, so you should confidently lead a spade from your king after taking your ruff.

11. Continue with the ♠K. Partner merely says he isn't too keen on a spade continuation. His signal does not compel you to switch. Another spade lead cannot cost (and could gain), while no switch is attractive. Note that dummy is weak, so you should not be eager to switch, desperately looking for tricks. A *low* card may be *noncommittal*, showing doubt.

12. *Duck* the ♠K. Perhaps partner has a singleton spade and can signal the location of his entry with his discard.

Lesson 7

COUNTING

Counting is among the most important elements of good defensive play. Unless you make counting a habit, you will soon discover that producing consistently good defense is impossible. In an earlier lesson, you learned that the defenders must count their tricks. The other aspects of counting on defense are just as vital. You must:

1. COUNT DECLARER'S DISTRIBUTION. The bidding oftens provides the first clue to declarer's distribution. Further information is available from partner's opening lead and count signals, and when partner and declarer fail to follow suit. Before long, you may have a *complete* count of declarer's distribution.
2. COUNT DECLARER'S HIGH-CARD POINTS. The bidding usually indicates about how many high-card points declarer has (if he opens 1 NT, for example). As the play proceeds, you can see what cards make up declarer's high-card strength — and deduce what cards your partner has.
3. COUNT DECLARER'S TRICKS. A count of declarer's possible tricks tells you whether you must adopt an active or passive approach on defense.

Although declarer only occasionally applies the technique of counting, the defenders must do their counting on virtually every deal.

65

1.

♠ Q 6
♥ 10 7 4 2
♦ Q 10 8 4
♣ Q 5 2

♠ 10 8 5
♥ 8 3
♦ A K 3
♣ J 10 9 7 3

South opened 1 ♥ and went to 4 ♥ after North raised to 2 ♥. You lead the ♣J, which holds. Declarer ruffs the next club and draws two rounds of trumps, your partner's jack falling on the second round. Next, declarer leads the ♠Q, a spade to his king and the ♠A. He ruffs a fourth round of spades in dummy, as partner plays the jack, and ruffs a club back to his hand. Declarer then leads a low diamond toward dummy. How do you defend?

2.

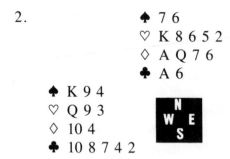

♠ 7 6
♥ K 8 6 5 2
♦ A Q 7 6
♣ A 6

♠ K 9 4
♥ Q 9 3
♦ 10 4
♣ 10 8 7 4 2

South opened 1 ♦, North responded 1 ♥; South rebid 1 ♠, North jumped to 3 ♦. South bid 3 NT. You lead the ♣4. Dummy plays the 6, and partner wins the king and returns the ♣3, declarer following low to both tricks. At trick three declarer leads a spade to his queen, and you win the king. How do you defend?

LET'S SEE NOW — DECLARER HAS 4♠ AND FROM THE LOOKS OF PARD'S LEAD, 3♦S. THAT'S 6 CARDS LEFT IN ♣S AND ♡S. 6 SPLITS 4-2 A LOT OF THE TIME. DOES WEST HAVE 4♡? NO. HE WOULD HAVE BID 1♡ OVER 1♦, NOT 1♠. SO, GIVE HIM 2♡S AND 4♣S. I HAVE 3♡, DUMMY HAS 4, SO GIVE PARD 4 ♡S. PARD HAS 3♣S, AND IT LOOKS LIKE 4♦S. SO, SHE HAS 2♠S. WAIT. THAT ADDS UP TO ONLY 12♣S. SHE MUST HAVE 3♣S. SO 3-3 IN CLUBS AND ♡S. DECLARER IS 4-3-3-3. SO IS PARD. NOW LET'S COUNT POINTS...

3.

        ♠ K J 8 5
        ♡ A 10 6 5
        ◇ J 4
        ♣ A 7 5

♠ 9 2
♡ Q 7 3
◇ K Q 9 5
♣ 10 8 4 2

South opened 1♠, North raised to 3♠, South bid 6♠. You lead the ◇ K. Declarer wins the ace and draws two rounds of trumps, your partner following. Next, declarer plays the ♣K and ♣A and ruffs a club in his hand. Declarer then exits with a diamond to your queen. How do you defend?

4.

♠ A 5
♡ 8 6 5
◇ K J 6 2
♣ A 10 9 4

♠ K 9 3
♡ A Q 10 7 3
◇ 8 7
♣ K J 5

You, East, opened 1 ♡. South overcalled 2 ◇, North raised to 4 ◇, South went on to 5 ◇. Partner leads the ♡ 2. You win the ace, and declarer drops the king. Declarer ruffs the next heart and draws two rounds of trumps, your partner following once. South ruffs dummy's last heart and leads the ♣Q from his hand, ducking in dummy. You win the ♣K. How do you defend?

5.

♠ 10 4
♡ A J 6
◇ Q 7 5 3
♣ K J 7 5

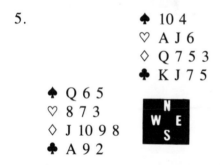

♠ Q 6 5
♡ 8 7 3
◇ J 10 9 8
♣ A 9 2

South opened 1 ♠, North responded 2 ♣; South rebid 2 ♡, North bid 2 NT; South tried 3 ♠, North raised to 4 ♠. You lead the ◇ J. Declarer wins the ace, plays off the A-K of trumps and leads another trump to your queen. Partner follows with the jack on the second trump and discards on the third. Declarer ruffs your diamond continuation and leads a club from his hand. Do you win or duck?

6.

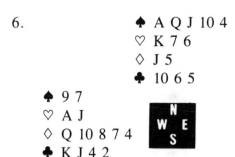

♠ A Q J 10 4
♡ K 7 6
◇ J 5
♣ 10 6 5

♠ 9 7
♡ A J
◇ Q 10 8 7 4
♣ K J 4 2

North opened 1 ♠, South responded 2 NT, North raised to 3 NT. You lead the ◇ 7, won by dummy's jack. Declarer then leads a heart to his queen. How do you defend?

7.

♠ Q 9 6 4
♡ Q 7 5
◇ A J 9 3
♣ J 3

♠ A 5
♡ 8 6 4 2
◇ K Q 4 2
♣ Q 10 7

South opened 1 ♠, North responded 2 ◇; South rebid 2 ♠, North raised to 3 ♠, South went on to 4 ♠. West leads the ♡J. Declarer wins in his hand with the ♡K and leads a trump to the queen and your ace. You return a heart to dummy's queen. Declarer draws another round of trumps, your partner following, cashes the ♡A and leads the ◇ 10, passing it to your queen. How do you defend?

8.
♠ K Q 6 4
♡ 8 5 3
◊ A 8 4
♣ K Q 5

♠ 7 5 2
♡ K J 9 4
◊ K 3
♣ 8 6 4 3

N
W E
S

North	South
1 ♣	1 ◊
1 ♠	3 ◊
4 ◊	4 NT
5 ◊	6 ◊

West leads the ♡2. You play the jack (you know declarer holds the ace), and declarer wins the queen. He leads the ◊ Q and finesses to your king. How do you defend?

SOLUTIONS

1. Play a low diamond. Declarer is known to have five hearts, four spades and one club, so he has three diamonds. If he lacks the ◇ J, he will probably finesse the ◇ 10. Note that you must do your counting in advance so you can play low without pause.

2. Declarer is marked with four clubs from partner's plays. (Partner would win the ♣ Q with K-Q-3 and would return the ♣ J with K-J-3.) Declarer bid spades and diamonds and should have four cards in each suit; so he has at most a singleton heart. Shift to the ♡ Q, in case declarer's singleton is the jack.

3. Declarer had five spades and two clubs. If he had three diamonds and three hearts, you can get out safely with a *diamond*. A diamond return is also safe if declarer had two diamonds and four hearts — a ruff-and-discard won't help him. A heart return runs an obvious risk, and a club return would give declarer a ruff-and-discard he *could* use if he had three diamonds and three hearts.

4. Count declarer's tricks. He has six diamonds and one spade. Even if you return a club and give him three club tricks, he is still a trick short and must lose a spade to you eventually. Any other return costs the contract, since declarer's hand is:

   ♠ Q x x x
   ♡ K
   ◇ A Q 10 x x x
   ♣ Q x

5. Play low, since declarer's pattern should be 6-4-1-2.

6. Declarer's 2 NT response promised 13-15 HCP. He has the ◇ A and ◇ K and the ♡ Q, and surely holds the ♠ K — if he lacked that card, he would lead spades, not hearts,

71

to set up his best suit. So declarer lacks the ♣A, and a club shift and return may net five tricks for the defense.

7. This is similar to hand #4. Declarer is known to have four spade tricks and three hearts. A diamond return will give him two tricks in diamonds, but he will still be a trick short unless he has the ♣A. A club return gives him a chance to make a hopeless contract if his hand is:

> ♠ K J 10 x x
> ♡ A K x
> ◇ 10 x
> ♣ K x x

(Declarer cannot hold ◇ 10xx and the doubleton ♣A; he would lead the ♣A and a club for a sure endplay.)

8. Declarer has at most six diamond tricks and two hearts. He can't make the contract if he lacks the ♠A (unless he happens to be void in spades), but he might make it without the ♣A, unless you lead a club. If declarer had four spade tricks, that would get him up to 12. Declarer's hand:

> ♠ A J x
> ♡ A Q
> ◇ Q J 10 x x x x
> ♣ x

Lesson 8

DEFENDERS' CARD COMBINATIONS; INFERRING CARD COMBINATIONS

The ability to *visualize* how cards in a suit lie around the table and what will happen when the suit is led is called *card sense*. All good card players possess this intangible quality. Card sense is especially important on defense, where only dummy is in view. Luckily, card sense can be acquired and developed.

We will deal with two areas of *card combinations on defense* in this lesson. First, the defenders often have card combinations that require correct handling. This may involve:

1. *Unblocking* a suit.
2. Keeping *communication* open.
3. Preserving an *entry*.
4. Making a *surrounding* play.
5. Other tactical plays.

QUIZ ON HANDLING DEFENDERS' CARD COMBINATIONS

1.

♠ 10 5
♡ Q 7 5
◇ K Q 10 6 5
♣ A 9 2

♠ Q 9 7 2
♡ J 9 2
◇ 8 7 4
♣ 10 8 6

South opened 1 NT, North raised to 3 NT. West leads the ♠ 4, and declarer wins your queen with the ace. Next declarer leads the ◇ J, won by partner's ace. Partner lays down the ♠ J. What card do you play?

2.

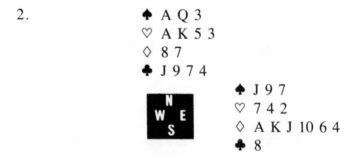

♠ A Q 3
♡ A K 5 3
◇ 8 7
♣ J 9 7 4

♠ J 9 7
♡ 7 4 2
◇ A K J 10 6 4
♣ 8

North opened 1 ♣, you overcalled 2 ◇ (weak), South jumped to 3 NT. West leads the ◇ 9. How do you defend?

3.
```
♠ 8 5 3
♡ K Q 10 7 6
◇ J 4
♣ A K J
```
```
        ♠ K Q 10 6 2
        ♡ A 8
        ◇ 7 6
        ♣ Q 7 5 3
```

North opened 1♡; you overcalled 1♠, South jumped to 3 NT. West leads the ♠J. What do you play? What would you play if your spades were K-Q-10-9-2?

4.
```
♠ 6 5 3
♡ 7 6
◇ K Q 10 7 6 3
♣ A 8
```
```
        ♠ K 7
        ♡ 10 8 5 3
        ◇ A 9 2
        ♣ K 10 9 7
```

South opened 1 NT, North raised to 3 NT. West leads the ♠Q. Plan your defense.

5.

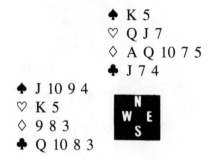

♠ K 5
♡ Q J 7
◇ A Q 10 7 5
♣ J 7 4

♠ J 10 9 4
♡ K 5
◇ 9 8 3
♣ Q 10 8 3

South opened 1 ♡, North responded 2 ◇. South rebid 2 ♡, North raised to 4 ♡. You lead the ♠ J. Dummy's king wins, and declarer passes the ♡ Q to your king. What do you lead now?

6.

♠ 10 5
♡ A K J 10 6 5
◇ K J 5
♣ 6 5

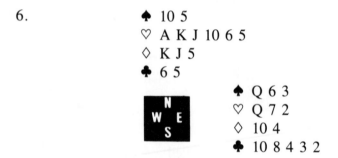

♠ Q 6 3
♡ Q 7 2
◇ 10 4
♣ 10 8 4 3 2

South opened 1 ♣, North responded 1 ♡. South rebid 1 ♠, North jumped to 3 ♡, South bid 3 NT. West leads the ◇ 9. Declarer wins the queen in his hand and leads a low heart to dummy's 10. How do you defend?

7.
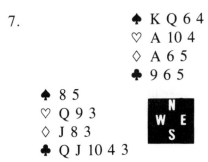

♠ K Q 6 4
♡ A 10 4
◇ A 6 5
♣ 9 6 5

♠ 8 5
♡ Q 9 3
◇ J 8 3
♣ Q J 10 4 3

Southopened 1♠, North raised to 3♠, South jumped to 6♠. You lead the ♣Q. Declarer wins the king, draws two rounds of trumps (partner following), and leads the king, ace and another diamond, ruffing in his hand. Declarer then cashes the ♣A and puts you in with a third round of clubs, as partner discards a diamond. What do you lead?

8.

♠ 9 6 4
♡ K J 10
◇ A Q 10 9 4
♣ K 4

♠ K 10 8 2
♡ A 4
◇ K 6 5
♣ 10 9 6 3

South opened 1♣, North responded 1◇. South rebid 1 NT, North raised to 3 NT. West leads the ♡9. How do you defend?

SOLUTIONS

1. Partner's play of the ♠J suggests that he is preparing to cash his spade tricks. You must be careful to *unblock* the 7 or 9 on this trick. Partner's spade suit is K-J-6-4-3. Note what happens if you fail to unblock.

2. Play your ◇10 at trick one, letting declarer win but keeping communication with partner. If partner has a doubleton

diamond and an entry, you can cash all your diamonds later. Keeping a link with partner is essential because you lack a side entry.

3. Play the ♠6. You can't afford to overtake partner's jack. (Declarer could have A-9-7-4, in which case overtaking would establish a second stopper for him.) If your suit were K-Q-10-9-2, to overtake would be mandatory in case the ♠J were a singleton.

4. First, you must overtake the ♠Q to get out of partner's way. If you play low, declarer can win the first spade, blocking the suit. If you overtake, however, declarer must duck, else your side cashes spades when you win your ◇A. If declarer lets your ♠K win, shift to the ♣K, attacking dummy's entry to the diamonds. If you can keep declarer from using his diamonds, the contract will surely fail. (To return partner's suit is fruitless because he cannot have a fast entry to his spades. A count of high-card points tells you that partner has at most a queen outside spades.)

5. It is clear to shift to clubs, but you must be careful to lead the 10, a *surrounding* play. The club situation is:

	J 7 4	
Q 10 8 3	■	K 6 2
	A 9 5	

Note what may happen if you lead low.

6. Shift to the ♠Q. Your best chance for five tricks is to find partner with the ♣A plus the ♠AJ9x. If you lead a low spade, declarer will duck the trick to partner, preventing your side from taking three fast spade tricks.

7. Assuming declarer has the ♠K and partner has the jack (the only time your play matters), you must lead the ♡Q. The heart position is:

```
            A 10 4
Q 9 3       ■           J 6 5 2
            K 8 7
```

Note the result if you lead the ♡3.

8. Win the ♡A and shift to the ♠10, a *surrounding* play. This is necessary if declarer holds ♠AJx and partner has ♠Qxx. Note what may happen if you lead low.

The second part of this lesson is *inferring* card combinations on defense.

If you can trust declarer to play logically, you can draw conclusions about his hand. Drawing inferences — assumptions based on the logical interpretation of evidence — is an essential part of reconstructing declarer's high cards, distribution and possible tricks.

Here are examples of inferring declarer's holding from his play:

You are defending 4♠. Declarer has drawn trumps, leaving some in dummy. Next, he attacks hearts.

```
              ♡ 7 5
♡ Q J 8 2     ■
```

He leads a heart from dummy to his 10, and you win the jack. Could declarer have 10-6-4-3? No, partner would have won with either the ace or king. Could declarer have K-10-3? No, he would have put up the king, hoping for only one heart loser. Declarer's most likely heart holding is A-10-x-(x).

You are defending a notrump contract. Declarer attacks hearts.

♡ A J 9 3

♡ Q 7 4 　　■

He leads a heart from hand and plays dummy's 9, losing to partner's 10. Clearly, your partner has the ♡ K, else declarer would have played the jack (or ace) from dummy.

QUIZ ON INFERRING CARD COMBINATIONS

I.　You are defending 4 ♡. Declarer has drawn trumps, leaving some in dummy. He then attacks the spade suit.

1.　　　　　　K J 9 4

　A 7 3　　■

He leads low to dummy's 9, losing to partner's 10. Who has the ♠ Q? How many spades does declarer have?

2.　　　　　　7 5

　Q 10 6　　■

He leads low from dummy to his 9, and you win the 10. Who has the ♠ A? Who has the ♠ K?

3.　　　　　　7 6

　A J 5 2　　■

He leads low from dummy and plays the 10 from hand, losing to your jack. Who has the ♠ Q? Who has the ♠ K?

4.   A 10 5
        K 7 6 2   ■

He leads low from dummy to his queen, your king winning.
Who has the ♠J?

In the remaining problems, the contract is *notrump*.

5.   A Q 7
        K 10 8 5 2   ■

You lead the ♠5, and declarer plays dummy's queen, winning the trick. Who has the ♠J?

6.   Q 5
        J 9 7 2   ■

You lead the ♠2, and declarer puts up dummy's queen. Partner covers with the king, and declarer's ace wins. Who is likely to have the ♠10?

7.   Q 5
                       ■   K 10 6 2

Partner leads the ♠4, and declarer plays low from dummy.
Who has the ♠A?

8.   J 5
                       ■   K 9 6 2

Partner leads the ♠3. Declarer plays low from dummy and
captures your king with his ace. Who has the ♠Q? Who has
the ♠10?

9.

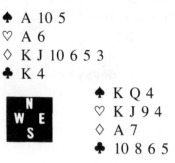

♠ A 10 5
♡ A 6
◇ K J 10 6 5 3
♣ K 4

♠ K Q 4
♡ K J 9 4
◇ A 7
♣ 10 8 6 5

North opened 1 ◇ , you doubled, South bid 1 NT, North raised to 2 NT, South went on to 3 NT. West leads the ♠ 3. Declarer plays the ace from dummy. What do you play on this trick?

10.

♠ K 9 5 3
♡ K 10 9 3
◇ 8 5
♣ J 9 6

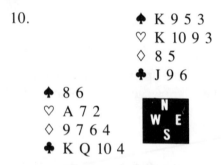

♠ 8 6
♡ A 7 2
◇ 9 7 6 4
♣ K Q 10 4

South opened 1 ♠ , and North raised to 2 ♠ , which became the contract. You lead the ♣ K. You find partner with A-x-x and you cash three tricks in the suit. Partner shifts to the ◇ Q, won by declarer's king. Declarer draws two rounds of trumps, your partner following, and leads a heart toward dummy. You play low, and declarer finesses dummy's 9, losing to partner's jack. Partner leads another diamond, won by declarer's ace. Now declarer leads a second heart toward dummy. Do you take your ace or duck again?

SOLUTIONS

1. Partner surely has the ♠Q. Declarer should have three or more spades. With only two spades, he would try for only one spade loser by playing the jack or king from dummy.

2. Declarer must have one of the high honors, since partner would *win the trick* with both the ace and king. If declarer had only the king, he would play it, hoping for one loser in the suit. So he should have the ace.

3. Declarer has one of the missing honors, since partner would *split* with the K-Q to assure one trick. But if declarer had only the king, he would play it, hoping for one loser in the suit. So declarer has the queen.

4. Partner has the ♠J, since declarer would take a finesse against your king if he held both the queen and jack.

5. Partner has the ♠J. If declarer held that card, he would duck the opening lead to his hand.

6. Partner is likely to have the ♠10, unless declarer's holding was specifically A-10 doubleton. If declarer's spades were A-10-x-(x), he could assure two tricks by playing low from dummy.

7. Partner is likely to have the ace. If declarer had ♠Axx or ♠AJx, he would put up the queen from dummy at trick one as his only chance to take a trick with that card. You should play the king because declarer's spade holding may be J-x.

8. If declarer had ♠AQx, he would play dummy's jack at trick one, hoping to save his A-Q tenace. If he had A-x-x, he would play the jack in desperation and might duck your king. His most likely holding is A-10-x.

9. Unblock one of your honors, hoping partner's spades are J-x-x-x-(x). If declarer had the ♠J, he would be tempted to duck the opening lead, saving his A-10 tenace in dummy and hoping for a second spade trick. (Perhaps declarer

took dummy's ♠ A immediately because he fears a heart switch, but he simply might have erred.)

10. Duck the second heart. If declarer had only two hearts, he would put up dummy's king on the first lead, hoping it would hold. If you duck the second heart smoothly, declarer may play dummy's 10 and lose to partner's queen. Of course, declarer should have cashed both of his diamonds before leading hearts (partner would be end-played when he won a heart trick). But part of winning bridge is taking advantage of the opponents' errors.

Lesson 9

MORE ABOUT INFERENCES

Bridge is a game of logic. A session consists of a series of little problems. Although basic tendencies and principles of play will solve many of these problems, some of the answers must be deduced.

An *inference* is a conclusion reached by analyzing evidence. You learned that the defenders can infer certain features of declarer's hand from the way he plays his card combinations. Other sources for useful inferences about declarer's hand are:

1. His approach to the play of the entire deal.
2. What happened (or didn't happen) in the bidding.
3. Your partner's opening lead and approach to the defense.

Through inferences, you can reconstruct declarer's high cards and distribution, a vital step in accurate defense.

In drawing inferences from an opponent's action, you must assume he is playing logically. It's wrong to act on a subtle inference, basing it on declarer's play, when your opponent is a poor player. (This is a good reason to play with and against stronger players. That's the way to improve!)

QUIZ ON DRAWING INFERENCES

1.
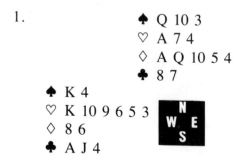

           ♠ Q 10 3
           ♡ A 7 4
           ◊ A Q 10 5 4
           ♣ 8 7

♠ K 4
♡ K 10 9 6 5 3
◊ 8 6
♣ A J 4

North opened 1 ◊ , South responded 1 ♠. You overcalled 2 ♡ . North raised to 2 ♠ , and South jumped to 4 ♠ . You lead the ♡ 10. Declarer wins dummy's ace and leads a spade to his ace and a spade back. You win the king, and partner's jack falls. What do you lead now?

2.
```
              ♠ 6 5
              ♡ A Q 6
              ◊ K 10 7 6 5
              ♣ K Q 5
♠ J 9 7 4 2
♡ K 5            N
◊ A 9 4 2     W     E
♣ A 10           S
```

North opened 1 ◊, South responded 2 ♣. North raised to 3 ♣, South jumped to 5 ♣. You lead the ♠ 4. Declarer takes partner's king with the ace and leads a trump from his hand. How do you defend?

3.
```
              ♠ J 10 7 5
              ♡ A 6 5 2
              ◊ 8 7
              ♣ 10 6 5
                            ♠ 9 6 4 2
                            ♡ K Q J 9
                N           ◊ A 6
             W     E        ♣ A 8 3
                S
```

South	West	North	East
1 ◊	Pass	1 ♡	Dbl
2 ◊	3 ♣	Pass	Pass
3 ◊	(All Pass)		

West leads the ♠ K. Declarer wins the ace and leads the ◊ K. How do you defend?

4.

♠ K J 10 6 4
♡ A Q J
◇ Q 10 5
♣ K 5

♠ A 5 2
♡ 9 8 7 5
◇ K 6
♣ A 10 6 3

North opened 1♠, South responded 1 NT. North raised to 2 NT, South went on to 3 NT. You lead the ♣3. Dummy plays low, East plays the 8 and declarer wins the 9. At trick two declarer leads a heart to the queen and your partner's king. Partner returns the ♣4. Declarer follows with the 7, and you win the ace. What do you lead?

5.

♠ Q 4
♡ K 7 5
◇ K J 9 7 6 3
♣ J 8

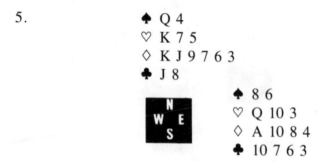

♠ 8 6
♡ Q 10 3
◇ A 10 8 4
♣ 10 7 6 3

South opened 1 NT, and North raised to 3 NT. West leads the ♡2. What is declarer's distribution?

6.

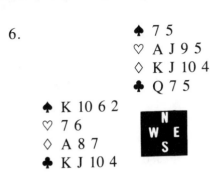

♠ 7 5
♡ A J 9 5
◇ K J 10 4
♣ Q 7 5

♠ K 10 6 2
♡ 7 6
◇ A 8 7
♣ K J 10 4

South	West	North	East
1 ♡	Dbl	Redbl	Pass
Pass	1 ♠	3 ♡	Pass
4 ♡	(All Pass)		

You lead a trump. Declarer wins and draws another round, your partner following low. Declarer then leads the ◇ Q, which you duck, and another diamond, which you win. What do you lead?

7.

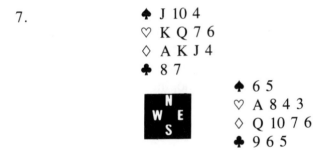

♠ J 10 4
♡ K Q 7 6
◇ A K J 4
♣ 8 7

♠ 6 5
♡ A 8 4 3
◇ Q 10 7 6
♣ 9 6 5

South opened 1 ♠, North responded 2 ◇. South rebid 2 NT, North tried 3 ♠, South went on to 4 ♠. West leads the ♡9. How do you defend when declarer puts up dummy's ♡K?

8.

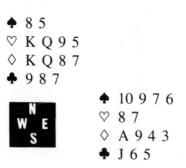

♠ 8 5
♥ K Q 9 5
♦ K Q 8 7
♣ 9 8 7

♠ 10 9 7 6
♥ 8 7
♦ A 9 4 3
♣ J 6 5

South opened 1 NT, North responded 2 ♣. South rebid 2 ♠, North bid 3 NT. South took out to 4 ♥, which became the contract. West leads the ♦ 10, and declarer plays the king from dummy. How do you defend?

SOLUTIONS

1. Lead a low heart. Partner must have the ♥ Q, since declarer would duck your lead to his hand if he started with Q-x. You hope partner can win and lead a club through declarer's holding.

2. Once partner shows the ♠ K, declarer must have every other face card to justify his leap to an 11-trick contract. Your only chance is to take your trump ace and lead the ♦ A and another diamond, hoping partner can trump. Declarer's hand:

♠ A Q x
♥ x
♦ Q J x
♣ J x x x x x

3. Partner should have the doubleton ♠ KQ! (If he led a spade from K-x, your chances are nil.) Suppose, instead, that partner had K-Q-x, leaving declarer with A-x. *Declarer would return a spade*, setting up a fast discard in dummy for a (heart) loser while he still had the ♥ A. (You can

assume that, with only two spades and not many clubs, declarer will have at least one heart loser.) If you return a spade, partner can put you back in with the ♣A, and you can give him a spade ruff. This is the only successful defense, since declarer's hand is:

♠ A x x
♡ x x
♢ K Q J 10 x x
♣ K Q

4. Return a low spade, or the ♠A and another. Partner is likely to have the ♠Q, since declarer hasn't attacked that suit. Declarer's hand:

♠ x
♡ 10 x x x
♢ A J 9 x
♣ Q J 9 x

If the defenders do not set up their fifth trick in spades, declarer will go after diamonds and make his contract.

5. Declarer has *three hearts*, judging by partner's opening lead. Declarer has *five spades*, since partner would lead from a five-card spade suit in preference to a four-card heart suit after this auction. Declarer has *three clubs* at least, since partner would also lead from a five-card club suit. But declarer must have at least two diamonds for his 1 NT opening. Declarer's pattern, therefore, is 5-3-2-3. Simple, isn't it?

6. You can infer that declarer has four spades, since partner would have bid 1 ♠ over North's redouble with four cards in that suit. (Even with a bad hand, partner would be duty-bound to confirm the best place to play.) You must lead a club. If declarer has losing clubs, they are about to go away on dummy's diamond winners. Notice that a club

shift can't lose even if declarer has the ace! — he would discard his clubs on the diamonds anyway. If partner has the ♣A, however, you must lead a club now. Because declarer has four spades, you can wait to lead a spade even if your partner has the ace. Declarer can throw only two of his spades on the diamonds.

7. Duck the first trick. Partner's ♡9 cannot be a singleton — declarer would have rebid 2♡, not 2 NT, with a four-card heart suit. Perhaps partner has a doubleton heart and a high trump for a reentry.

8. Duck the first trick. Partner's lead cannot be a singleton — that would mean declarer has four diamonds, four hearts, four spades and a singleton club for his 1 NT opening! Perhaps partner has a doubleton diamond, plus the ace of trumps for a reentry.

Lesson 10

FALSE CARDS;
DECEPTION ON DEFENSE

Falsecarding and deception are fascinating aspects of defensive play. However, many players are so eager to be tricky that they overdo it. The first rule of deceptive defense is:

Avoid frivolous false cards. Make your deceptive plays purposeful. Don't be the kind of player who tosses out cards at random.

An ideal false card fools the opponents without fatally misleading partner. Random false cards with no purpose accomplish nothing.

If your partner is a poor player and never pays attention to your carding, you can get away with anything. Otherwise, feed your partner honest information unless you have a reason for deceptive play.

A *false card* offers an opponent a losing option in the play or diverts him from making the winning play. A basic principle in many falsecarding situations is:

> Keep your opponent guessing by playing a card you are already known to hold (or will soon be known to hold).

Look at this example:

```
              K J 5
   Q 10 4                  8 6 3
              A 9 7 2
```

Declarer, who needs four tricks from this suit, finesses dummy's jack successfully. When dummy leads the king next, West must drop his queen, the card declarer knows he holds. Declarer now has the losing option of leading to his 9 on the third round, playing West for Q-4 and East for 10-8-6-3. If West does not falsecard, declarer cannot go wrong — this, therefore, is a so-called *obligatory* false card.

QUIZ ON FALSE CARDS

1.

♠ 6 4 3
♡ Q 9 4
◊ A K 7 6 5
♣ A 6

♠ K 9 5
♡ K 10
◊ J 8 2
♣ Q 10 4 3 2

South opened 1 ♡, North responded 2 ◊. South rebid 2 NT, North jumped to 4 ♡. West leads the ♠ 2. Declarer wins your ♠ K with the ace, leads a club to dummy's ace and a heart from dummy. What do you play?

2.

♠ A Q 6 4
♡ 5 3
◊ K Q 8 6
♣ 8 7 6

♠ 10 9 3
♡ K 9 6 4
◊ J 3 2
♣ K 5 2

South opened 1 NT, North responded 2 ♣. South rebid 2 ♠, North raised to 4 ♠. West leads the ♣ J, won by declarer's queen. At trick two declarer leads a low spade to dummy's queen. What do you play?

3.

♠ 7 3
♡ K J
◇ A K Q 6 4
♣ J 7 6 5

♠ A K J 4
♡ Q 10 8 2
◇ 8 7 5
♣ 9 3

South opened 1 ♡ , North responded 2 ◇ . South rebid 2 ♡ , North jumped to 4 ♡ . You lead the ♠ A and cash the ♠ K, declarer following low. Declarer wins your ♣ 9 shift with the 10 and leads a low heart toward dummy. What do you play?

4.

♠ Q 8 5
♡ A K J 10 4
◇ K 7 6
♣ 8 7

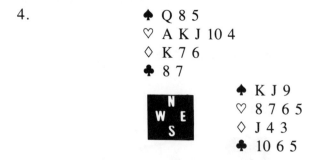

♠ K J 9
♡ 8 7 6 5
◇ J 4 3
♣ 10 6 5

South opened 1 ♠ , North responded 2 ♡ . South rebid 2 NT, North jumped to 4 ♠ . West cashes the ♣ A and ♣ K and shifts to the ◇ 10, won by dummy's king. Declarer then leads a low trump from dummy. What do you play?

5. ♠ A Q 7 6 3
    ♡ K 7 6
    ◇ A J 7
    ♣ 10 4

♠ K J 9
♡ Q 10 5 3
◇ 9 8
♣ K Q 9 5

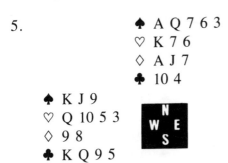

North opened 1 ♠, South responded 2 ♣. North rebid 2 ♠, South tried 2 NT, North raised to 3 NT. You lead the ♡ 3. Partner plays the jack, and declarer wins the ace. Declarer then leads a spade to dummy's queen and continues with the ♠ A. What do you play?

6. ♠ Q 8 6 5 2
    ♡ K 7 6
    ◇ A 8 7
    ♣ A 5

♠ K J 9
♡ Q 10 8 3 2
◇ J 6
♣ K J 4

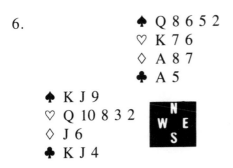

North opened 1 ♠, South responded 1 NT and all passed. You lead the ♡ 3. Partner plays the jack, and declarer wins the ace. Next, declarer lays down the ♠ A — not the card you wanted to see. What do you play?

7.

♠ K 10 8
♡ J 6 4
◇ A 8 7 5
♣ 6 5 4

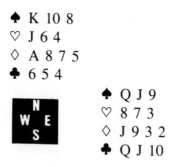

♠ Q J 9
♡ 8 7 3
◇ J 9 3 2
♣ Q J 10

South opened 1 ♡, North raised to 2 ♡, South jumped to 4 ♡. West leads the ◇ K. Declarer wins dummy's ace, draws trumps and leads a spade toward dummy. Partner plays low, and declarer inserts dummy's 8. How do you defend?

8.

♠ A 10 8 5
♡ K 6
◇ 10 9 5 3
♣ A 8 4

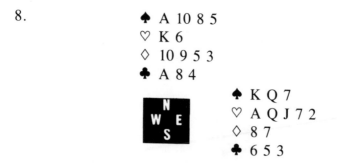

♠ K Q 7
♡ A Q J 7 2
◇ 8 7
♣ 6 5 3

South opened 1 ◇, North responded 1 ♠. South rebid 1 NT, North raised to 2 NT and everyone passed. West leads the ♠2. Declarer plays low from dummy. What do you play?

SOLUTIONS

1. Play the *king*. Declarer is likely to have A-J-x-x-x. He will win his ace and lead to dummy's 9, playing you for the singleton king and partner for 10-x-x-x. If, as expected, declarer has the missing heart honors, a false card is your only chance to win a trick.

2. Play the 9 (or 10). If your partner has the king of trumps, declarer will be tempted to come back to his hand and lead the jack, hoping to pin the doubleton 10-9 in your hand.

3. Play the *8*. Declarer may then play you for the singleton 8 or doubleton 10-8 by winning dummy's king and leading the jack.

4. Play the *jack*. This will cost nothing if partner has the 10. If declarer's spades are A-10-x-x-x, he will win and lead low to dummy's 8 on the second round, playing you for the singleton jack or the doubleton K-J.

5. Drop the *king*, the card you are known to hold. You hope to persuade declarer that the spades are not splitting evenly. Perhaps he will switch to clubs.

6. Drop your ♠K under the ace. Declarer may think the spades are breaking badly and look for tricks elsewhere.

7. Win the *jack*. Declarer must have three or more spades to play the suit this way. (With a doubleton spade, he would go up with dummy's king, hoping for one loser in the suit.) If you win the 9, declarer will have no option but to play the king on the next spade lead. If you win the jack, he has a losing option — he can lead to the *10* next.

8. You must fool *partner* to direct the defense. Since you badly want a heart shift, you must make him think no future lies in spades. Win the first trick with the ♠K, denying the queen. If partner gets in, he will shift, probably to a heart.

Aside from the standard falsecarding positions, the defenders have many other chances to lead declarer astray. Some deceptive techniques are:

---

1. Letting declarer win the first time he tries a repeatable finesse.
2. Winning a trick with a higher card than necessary.
3. Declining to cash a winner at the first opportunity.
4. Underleading winners or intermediates to make declarer guess.
5. Ducking deceptively.

Again, remember that a deceptive play must have a purpose. Do not play deceptive cards at random.

QUIZ ON DECEPTION ON DEFENSE

1.
                     ♠ 5
                     ♡ A K Q 5
                     ◇ K 7 5 3
                     ♣ A 8 6 4
        ♠ A 7 4
        ♡ J 7 4   N
        ◇ Q J 10   W   E
        ♣ J 9 5 3   S

South opened 3 ♠, North raised to 4 ♠. You lead the ◇ Q, winning the first trick. Your ◇ J holds the second trick, but declarer ruffs the third diamond. He then leads a heart to dummy and a spade toward his hand. Partner plays the 10, declarer the king. How do you defend?

2.

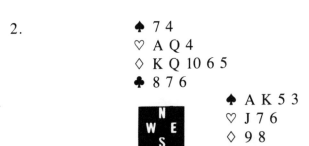

♠ 7 4
♡ A Q 4
◇ K Q 10 6 5
♣ 8 7 6

♠ A K 5 3
♡ J 7 6
◇ 9 8
♣ J 9 5 2

South opened 1 NT, North raised to 3 NT. West leads the ♠2. How do you defend?

3.

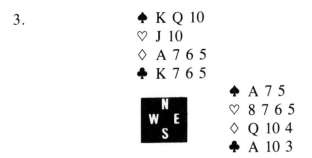

♠ K Q 10
♡ J 10
◇ A 7 6 5
♣ K 7 6 5

♠ A 7 5
♡ 8 7 6 5
◇ Q 10 4
♣ A 10 3

South opened 1 ♣, North raised to 3 ♣, South bid 3 NT. West leads the ♠ 2, and declarer plays the king from dummy. How do you defend?

4.
                    ♠ 5
                    ♡ Q 9 5
                    ◊ J 8 6 5
                    ♣ K 8 7 6 5

♠ Q J 10 8 4
♡ K 4 3
◊ A 7 3
♣ A 4

South opened 1 ♡ , you overcalled 1 ♠ . North raised to 2 ♡ , East jumped to 3 ♠ (*preemptive*, as you play), South bid 4 ♡ and everyone passed. You lead the ♠ Q. Partner plays the ♠ 7, and declarer wins the ace. Declarer ruffs the ♠ 9 in dummy and leads the ♡ Q, playing low from his hand. How do you defend?

5.
                    ♠ 6 5
                    ♡ J 4 3 2
                    ◊ 8 7 6 5 4
                    ♣ A K

♠ A Q
♡ 10 8 6 5
◊ J 3
♣ Q J 10 8 5

South opened 1 ♠ , North responded 1 NT; South rebid 3 ♠ , North raised to 4 ♠ . You lead the ♣ Q. Dummy wins, and declarer continues with a trump to his jack. How do you defend?

6.   ♠ A K J
                      ♡ Q 6 5
                      ◊ 6 5
                      ♣ A Q 10 7 6
  ♠ Q 6 5
  ♡ 10 9 8 7   **N**
  ◊ A 10 4   **W   E**
  ♣ J 5 3   **S**

   South opened 1 NT, North raised to 6 NT. You lead the ♡ 10.
Declarer wins the jack in his hand, goes to the ♣ Q and leads
a diamond to his king. How do you defend?

SOLUTIONS

1.   Duck smoothly. Partner may have the doubleton J-10 of
     trumps. If you duck, declarer must guess how to continue.
     He may lead a *low* spade next, hoping to bring down the
     ace. Note that if you win the first spade, declarer has no
     option but to bang down the queen later.
2.   Win the ♠ A and return the ♠ 3, putting declarer to a tough
     guess if his spades are Q-10-x. This play cannot cost, since
     declarer is known to have at least three spades from part-
     ner's lead of the *2*.
3.   In this position you almost always play *low* without think-
     ing. You hope partner has the jack. When the suit is led
     again, declarer must guess whether to play the queen or
     10 from dummy. Declarer has no chance to go wrong if
     you win the first spade.
4.   *Duck* the first heart (without pause, if you can). A forc-
     ing defense is your best chance, but if you win the first
     heart, dummy still has a trump to ruff a spade lead. If
     declarer takes a second heart finesse, however, you can
     win and force him to ruff *in his hand*. Since you still have
     two entries, you can gain control — you'll get in twice

to exhaust declarer's trumps with a spade lead and cash a spade.

5. Win the ♠A(!) and return a club. You hope to persuade declarer to use his last entry to dummy for another *spade* finesse. If you win the ♠Q, declarer will use the remaining entry to take a possible finesse in a red suit. Declarer's hand is:

    ♠ K J 10 x x x x
    ♡ K Q
    ◊ A Q
    ♣ x x

6. On the bidding, there is just enough room for partner to have the ◊J. (He must hold that card for the defense to have a chance.) If you win the first diamond, declarer will know he can take only one diamond trick. He will be forced to take the spade finesse for his 12th trick, and you know it will work. You can make a second diamond lead attractive by *ducking the first diamond*. Now declarer has no reason to try the spades. He will probably go back to dummy and lead a second diamond to his queen. You win and return a diamond to partner's jack. Declarer's hand is:

    ♠ x x x
    ♡ A K J
    ◊ K Q x
    ♣ K x x x

Note that you must duck the first diamond *smoothly*.

COMPREHENSIVE GLOSSARY

"ABOVE THE LINE": Scoring of points won for overtricks, penalties and bonuses.

ACTIVE DEFENSE: The defenders' approach when they are desperate for tricks because declarer threatens to get discards for his losers.

ASSUMPTION: Technique by which declarer or a defender bases his play on the premise that the contract can be made or set.

ATTITUDE: Defensive signal that shows like or dislike for a suit.

AVOIDANCE: Technique in play whereby a dangerous opponent is kept from gaining the lead.

AUCTION: See BIDDING.

BALANCED HAND: Hand containing no void suit or singleton, and no more than one doubleton.

BALANCING: Backing into the auction after the opponents have stopped low, counting on partner to hold some values.

"BELOW THE LINE": Scoring of points that count toward making a game.

BID: Call in the auction that promises to take a certain number of tricks in the play and suggests a suit as trumps (or suggests the play be at notrump).

BIDDING: The first phase of each hand of bridge, when the players on both sides have a chance to name the trump suit and suggest how many tricks they expect their side to win in the play.

BLACKWOOD:	A conventional bid of 4 NT that asks partner to reveal, through an artificial response, the number of aces he holds.
BOOK:	(1) The first six tricks won by declarer's side; (2) the number of tricks the defenders must win before they begin to score undertricks.
BROKEN SEQUENCE:	Sequence such as QJ9, which contains a gap between the middle and lowest of the three cards.
BROKEN SUIT:	Suit that contains no cards adjacent in rank.
BUSINESS DOUBLE:	Penalty double.
CALL:	Any action, including a pass, taken in the bidding.
CAPTAINCY:	The bidding principle whereby one partner is obliged to take responsibility for placing the contract once his partner's hand is limited in strength.
CARD SENSE:	An intangible quality that those skilled in card play seem to possess.
CHICAGO SCORING:	A type of scoring in which every deal is taken as a separate entity. There are no rubbers or partscores carried over to the next deal.
COME-ON:	An encouraging attitude signal.
COMPETITIVE BIDDING:	Auctions in which both sides bid.

CONSTRUCTIVE BIDDING: Auctions in which one side tries to reach its best contract without interference.

CONTRACT: The number of tricks the side that wins the auction undertakes to make.

CONTROL: Holding that prevents the opponents from taking two fast tricks in that suit. An ace; king; or singleton or void, if some other suit is trumps.

CONVENTION: A bid to which an artificial meaning is assigned.

CROSS-RUFF: A play technique in which cards are trumped in both partnership hands alternately on several successive tricks.

CUEBID: (1) A bid of an opponent's suit, intended to show great strength.
(2) A bid of a suit in which a control is held, intended to facilitate slam investigation.
(3) Any of several conventional cuebids, such as Michaels.

CUT: The division of the pack into rough halves prior to the deal.

DEAL: The distribution of the 52 cards, 13 to each player face down, that begins each hand of bridge.

DECLARER: The player who tries to make the contract by using both his own and dummy's cards.

DEFENDERS: The partnership that opposes declarer and tries to defeat the contract.

DISCARD:	A played card that is not of the suit led nor of the trump suit.
DOUBLE FINESSE:	A combination of plays in which declarer finesses against two missing honors.
DOUBLE SQUEEZE:	An advanced type of squeeze in which each defender is squeezed in turn.
DOUBLETON:	A holding of two cards in a suit.
DOUBLE:	A call generally intended to increase the penalty suffered by the opponents if their last bid becomes an unsuccessful contract.
DRAW TRUMPS:	Technique in which declarer leads trumps, forcing the opponents to follow suit, until their trumps are exhausted.
DROP:	Cause a missing high card to fall by playing a still higher card or cards.
DUMMY:	Declarer's partner. The term is also applied to the dummy's cards, placed face up on the table.
DUMMY REVERSAL:	Technique by which declarer makes extra tricks by ruffing several times in his own hand and ultimately drawing trumps with dummy's trump holding.
DUPLICATE BRIDGE:	A contest in which the same hands are played several times by different players, allowing for a comparison of results.
DUPLICATION OF VALUES:	The condition in which the high cards and distribution of the partnership hands are ill-suited to each other.
ECHO:	A high-low sequence of play used by a defender to signal attitude or count.

ENDPLAY:	Technique by which a trick is gained through deliberately giving an opponent the lead in a position where he has no safe exit.
ENTRY:	A card used as a means of gaining the lead.
EQUALS:	Cards that are adjacent in rank, or that become adjacent when the cards that separate them are played.
FALSE CARD:	A card played with intent to deceive.
FALSE PREFERENCE:	A preference offered without true support, typically with two cards.
FINESSE:	Maneuver by which it is hoped to win a trick with an intermediate card, by playing that card after one opponent has already played.
FIT:	A holding that suggests the suit will adequately serve as trumps.
FIVE-CARD MAJORS:	A bidding style in which an opening bid of 1♠ or 1♡ promises five or more cards.
FOLLOWING SUIT:	Each player's first obligation in the play, to play a card of the same suit that was led to the trick if possible.
FORCING BID:	A bid that compels partner to take further action.
FORCING DEFENSE:	The defenders' approach when they try to exhaust declarer of his trumps by repeatedly forcing him to ruff.

FORCING PASS:	Pass made over an opponent's bid, which compels partner to double the opponents or bid further.
FREE BID:	Bid made when the alternative would be to pass and allow partner the next opportunity to act. Typically based on sound values.
FREE RAISE:	Raise of partner's suit in competition. Not a significant term, since such a raise does *not* imply extra strength.
GAME:	(1) A unit of scoring, two of which comprise a rubber; a game is won by the first partnership to score 100 or more points below the line. (2) Any contract that will allow the partnership to score game if fulfilled.
GAME TRY:	A bid that suggests interest in game and asks partner to assess his values and make the final decision.
GERBER:	A conventional bid of 4 ♣ that asks partner to reveal, through an artificial response, the number of aces he holds.
GRAND SLAM FORCE:	A bid of 5 NT, when used to show interest in bidding a grand slam in the agreed trump suit provided partner holds certain honors in trumps.
HIGH-CARD POINT COUNT:	Method of hand evaluation in which a numerical value is assigned to each high honor.
HONOR:	Ace, king, queen, jack or ten.

HONORS:	Bonus available in the scoring for a holding of four or all five honors in the trump suit in the same hand; or, at notrump, all four aces in the same hand.
HOLD-UP:	Refusal to take a winner, often for purposes of disrupting the opponents' communication.
INFERENCE:	A conclusion logically deduced from evidence.
INFERENTIAL COUNT:	An assessment of the entire distribution of the concealed hands, based on evidence from the bidding and the early play.
INTERIOR SEQUENCE:	Holding such as KJ109x, in which the equals are accompanied by a higher honor.
INTERMEDIATES:	Cards that may become winners as the cards that outrank them are played.
INVITATIONAL BID:	Bid that asks partner to continue to game or slam with maximum values.
JORDAN:	The conventional understanding in which a jump to 2 NT by responder, after the opening bid is doubled for takeout, shows a limit raise in opener's suit.
JUMP OVERCALL:	A suit bid usually made (as the next bid) after an opponent has opened the bidding, but at a higher level than necessary.
JUMP SHIFT:	(1) A jump of one level in a new suit by opening bidder. (2) A jump of one level in a new suit by responder. Either action implies great strength.

LEG:	A fulfilled partscore, a step toward game.
LEAD:	The first card played to a trick.
LIMIT BID:	Bid that promises no more than a pre-agreed amount of high-card strength.
LIMIT RAISE:	Direct double raise of partner's opening one-bid that promises invitational values only.
LONG CARDS:	Low cards that become winners because they are the only cards of their suit that remain in play.
MAJOR SUITS:	Spades and hearts.
MATCHPOINT SCORING:	Type of scoring used in duplicate (tournament) bridge, in which several different results from an identical deal are compared.
MAXIMUM:	Holding the greatest possible values for one's previous bidding.
MINIMUM:	Holding the fewest possible values for one's previous bidding.
NEGATIVE RESPONSE:	Bid, often artificial, that denies good values; made in response to partner's forcing action.
NOTRUMP:	Strain in which the play is conducted with no trump suit. The highest card played of the suit that is led to a trick wins that trick.
OBLIGATORY FALSECARD:	Falsecard that will lead to a certain loss if not played.

OBLIGATORY FINESSE:	The handling of certain suit combinations in which declarer plays a low card from both hands, hoping his opponent will be forced to follow suit with a high honor.
OFFSIDE:	Unfavorably placed for a finesse to work.
ONSIDE:	Favorably placed for a finesse to work.
OPEN THE BIDDING:	To make the first bid in the auction.
OPENING LEAD:	The lead to the first trick, made by the defender to declarer's left.
OVERCALL:	Bid in a suit after the opponents have opened the bidding (but before partner has taken any action).
OVERTRICKS:	Tricks taken in excess of those bid.
PARTIAL:	A partscore.
PARTNERSHIP:	Two players working as a unit. Bridge is played by two competing partnerships. Partners sit opposite each other. Trust and cooperation between partners are important features of the game.
PARTSCORE:	A contract below the level of game. Successful partscores can accumulate toward scoring game.
PASS:	Call in the auction when the player does not wish to bid, double or redouble.
PASSED OUT:	Deal on which none of the four players bid. Calls for another deal.
PASSIVE DEFENSE:	Defenders' approach when dummy is short of winners and the defense can wait on its tricks.

PENALTY DOUBLE:	Double made for a larger penalty, in the expectation that the contract will fail.
PERCENTAGE PLAY:	Line of play that will succeed most often, determined on only a mathematical basis.
PLAIN SUIT:	Any suit other than trumps.
POINT COUNT:	The method of hand evaluation whereby a numerical value is assigned to the possible trick-taking features of a hand.
POSITIVE RESPONSE:	Response to partner's forcing opening that promises certain good values.
PREEMPTIVE BID:	Bid made not for constructive purposes but merely to crowd the opponents and make it hard for them to bid accurately.
PREFERENCE:	A bid that chooses between two possible strains partner has offered.
PREPARED BID:	An opening bid in a low-ranking suit (often, a suit of only three cards), made so that a higher-ranking suit will provide an easy, space-saving rebid.
PRIMARY VALUES:	Aces and kings.
PROPRIETIES:	That section of the Laws of Contract Bridge that deals with ethics and etiquette.
PSYCHIC BID:	A bluff bid, made on a non-existent suit or without values, intended to intimidate the opposition.

QUANTITATIVE SLAM (GAME) TRY:	Bid that asks partner to pass or bid on, based strictly on the number of high-card values he holds .
RAISE:	A bid in the same suit (or notrump) that partner has just bid, often confirming that suit as trumps.
REBID:	(1) Bid the same suit a second time. (2) Any bid chosen at one's second turn.
REDOUBLE:	Call available in the auction that doubles, in turn, points scored if the contract is played doubled.
RESPONDER:	Opening bidder's partner.
RESTRICTED CHOICE:	A mathematical concept, based on the opponents' possible play from a holding of several equal cards, that may be helpful in determining the play of certain suit combinations.
REVERSE:	(1) A rebid in a new suit, such that the level of the contract will be increased if partner shows a preference for the first suit. (2) To bid in such a way, thereby showing a strong hand.
REVOKE:	Failure to follow suit when holding a card of the suit led.
RUBBER:	Unit of scoring in bridge, won by the side to first make two games, and carrying a large bonus.
RUFF:	To trump.

RUFF-AND-DISCARD (RUFF-SLUFF):	The lead of a suit in which both declarer and dummy are void, allowing declarer to discard a loser from the hand of his choice while he ruffs in the other.
RULE OF 11:	Device, applicable if the lead is known to be fourth highest, that may be used to make judgments in the play. Subtract the rank of the spot led from 11. The remainder shows the number of higher cards held by the hands, other than leader's.
SACRIFICE:	A deliberate overbid, but one in which declarer expects to be penalized fewer points than the opponents would score if allowed to play their own contract.
SAFETY PLAY:	The handling of a combination of cards so as to insure against a devastating loss of tricks.
SECOND HAND:	(1) The next player to have a chance to bid after the dealer. (2) The player who plays immediately after a trick is led to.
SECONDARY VALUES:	Queens and jacks.
SEMI-BALANCED HAND:	Hand which is neither balanced nor unbalanced by definition. 2-2-4-5 or 2-2-3-6 pattern.
SEQUENCE:	Three or more cards adjacent in rank, the highest one of which is an honor.
SET:	To defeat the contract.
SHORT CLUB:	See PREPARED BID.

SHUTOUT BID:	A preemptive bid.
SIGNAL:	Any of several conventional understandings through which the defenders can give each other information by means of the card they play.
SIGNOFF:	Bid suggesting that partner pass.
SIMPLE SQUEEZE:	Type of squeeze in which a single opponent is squeezed.
SINGLETON:	A holding of only one card in a suit.
SLAM:	A contract for 12 or 13 tricks, carrying a bonus in the scoring.
SPOT CARD:	Card below the rank of an honor.
SQUEEZE:	Technique, most often used by declarer, in which a defender is forced to relinquish a winner no matter what card he chooses.
STANDARD AMERICAN:	The bidding system most commonly used in America; essentially, the Goren style, with gadgets and refinements added.
STOPPER:	A card or combination of cards that threatens to produce a trick in a suit.
STRIP:	Play a suit or suits so as to make it impossible for an opponent to lead that suit or lead it safely.
SUIT-PREFERENCE SIGNAL:	Defensive signal that bears no relation to its own suit but shows interest in another, specific suit.

SURROUNDING PLAY:	Maneuver in which a defender breaks a suit by leading a high card that is part of a near-sequential holding.
SYSTEM:	The total framework in which the partnership assigns well-defined meanings to its bids and bidding sequences.
TABLE PRESENCE:	The ability to draw inferences from the extraneous things that happen at the table.
TAKEOUT DOUBLE:	Double that requests partner not to pass but to choose a suit (or notrump) to play in.
TEMPORIZE:	Bid a suit (often, an unplayable suit), in the expectation of supporting partner's suit later. May be required if no immediate raise is appropriate.
TENACE:	An honor or combination of honors that will be most valuable if the holder is fourth hand to play; e.g., AQ, KJ.
THIRD HAND:	In the auction, dealer's partner. In the play, leader's partner.
THIRD-SEAT OPENING:	An opening bid after two passes that may be based on sub-minimum values. Often it is intended as mainly lead-directing and mildly preemptive.
THROW-IN:	See ENDPLAY.
TRAP PASS:	Pass made with substantial values, including strength in the opponent's suit, in the hope of making a successful penalty double later.

TREATMENT:	A particular way of assigning a natural meaning to a bid or sequence of bids.
TRICK:	Four cards played in sequence, one by each player at the table, going clockwise.
TRUMPS:	The suit determined in the bidding to be that of the contract.
TRUMP CONTROL:	Technique by which declarer makes possession of the trump suit work to his advantage, exhausting the opponents of their trumps so he can safely establish and cash other winners.
TRUMP COUP:	The advanced play by which declarer can avoid losing a trick to an outstanding trump honor by forcing a defender to ruff and be overruffed.
TRUMP ECHO:	The high-low sequence of play in the trump suit, used in defense to show an odd number of trumps.
TRUMP PROMOTION:	Defensive technique in which declarer is forced to either ruff low and be overruffed or ruff high at the later cost of a trump trick.
TRUMP SUPPORT:	Usually four or more cards in partner's suit. Under some circumstances, three or fewer cards.
UNBALANCED HAND:	Hand containing a void suit or singleton.
UNBLOCK:	Play by declarer or defenders so as to allow the uninterrupted run of a long suit by proper management of the smaller cards.

UNDERTRICKS: Tricks that declarer has bid but fails to take.

UPPERCUT: Defensive technique in which a defender ruffs in with a trump intermediate and declarer is obliged to weaken his trump holding by overruffing.

VOID: A suit in which no cards are held.

VULNERABILITY: Condition in the scoring, achieved when one game is won toward completion of the rubber.

WEAK TWO-BID: Modern treatment in which an opening bid of 2 ♠, 2 ♡ or 2 ◊ shows a good six-card suit and about an average hand in high cards.

*END OF
THE GLOSSARY*

WHAT THE PROPRIETIES ARE ABOUT:

In a game such as poker, all sorts of gamesmanship is allowed. In bridge, *skill in choosing a bid or play is emphasized.* A strict code of ethics and courtesy is part of the game. The better the players in the game, the higher the standard of ethics is likely to be. A higher standard of ethics is demanded in tournament play than in a social game at home. The purpose of the *Proprieties,* that section of the Laws of bridge that deals with conduct and ethics, is to make the game more enjoyable for everyone, no matter what the situation.

Please take time to read these excerpts from the Proprieties, excerpted from the *Laws of Duplicate Contract Bridge* (1975 edition). If you observe the principles set down here, you will find yourself respected as both a partner and an opponent.

CONDUCT AND ETIQUETTE

A player should maintain at all times a courteous attitude toward his partner and the opponents. He should carefully avoid any remark or action that might cause annoyance or embarrassment to another player, or that might interfere with another player's enjoyment of the game.

As a matter of courtesy, a player should refrain from:

> Paying insufficient attention;
> Making gratuitous comments during the play as to the auction or the adequacy of the contract;
> Detaching a card from his hand before it is his turn to play;
> Arranging the cards he has played to previous tricks in a disorderly manner or mixing his cards together before the result of the deal has been agreed to;
> Making a questionable claim or concession; or
> Prolonging the play unnecessarily.

It is a breach of the Proprieties to:

Use different designations for the same call ("A
   Club," "I'll bid a club," etc., are incorrect. "One
   club" is the only proper form).

Indicate any approval or disapproval of a call or play.

Indicate the expectation or intention of winning or
   losing a trick before play to that trick has been
   completed.

Comment or act during the auction or play to call
   attention to a significant incident thereof, or to the
   state of the score, or to the number of tricks that
   will be required for success.

Look intently at any other player during the auction or
   play, or at another player's hand for the purpose of
   seeing his cards or observing the place from which
   he draws a card.

Vary the normal tempo of bidding or play for the
   purpose of disconcerting the other players.

COMMUNICATIONS BETWEEN PARTNERS:

Communication between partners during the auction and play
should be effected only by means of the calls and plays
themselves. Calls should be made in a uniform tone without
special emphasis or inflection, and without undue haste or
hesitation. Plays should be made without emphasis, gesture or
mannerism, and so far as possible, at a uniform rate.

It is improper for communication between partners to be effected through the *manner* in which calls and plays are made,
through extraneous remarks or gestures, or through questions
asked of the opponents or explanations given to them. When
a player has available to him improper information from his
partner's remark, question, explanation, gesture, mannerism,
special emphasis, inflection, haste or hesitation, *he should*

carefully avoid taking any advantage that might accrue to his side.

It is improper to have special understandings with partner regarding your bids and plays of which the opponents are unaware. The opponents are entitled to know about that fancy new bidding convention you and partner had decided to try out, and you are obliged to announce it to them before the game starts.

A NOTE ON PARTNERSHIP RAPPORT:

There are many bridge players who look on partner as a necessary evil, but your success at the bridge table will depend in great part on how well your partner performs. *Everything* that happens within your partnership can affect what kind of results you get, so your partner's morale should be important to you.

Nobody likes harsh criticism under any circumstances, but for people who play bridge seriously, the game is a real ego trip. We are sensitive about our game and our mistakes. If you point out your partner's errors right at the table (or, worse, if you are downright abusive), you won't accomplish anything constructive. On the contrary, you will probably get partner to dwell on his errors and induce him to play even worse.

A partnership at bridge is two people trying to act as one in an emotionally-charged setting. Recognize that when one player criticizes his partner, it is because he views partner's error as a direct reflection on his own ability; his ego has been ruffled.

You should always assume that your partner wants to win as badly as you do, and he is trying as hard as he can. Therefore, withold any criticism until after the game. Instead, you should be interested in *building* up his ego. If he makes an error, tell him that you would probably have done the same thing under the circumstances; or that he surely had what he thought was a good reason at the time he made his misguided bid or play.

Give his ego a chance to recover and he will play harder for the rest of the game.

Do your partner, your partnership and yourself a favor. Apply the Golden Rule when your partner makes an error.

NOTES

NOTES

NOTES

DEVYN PRESS PUBLICATIONS
BRIDGE BOOKS